FINDING MY PLACE

Minority Teens Write About College

By Youth Communication

Edited by Autumn Spanne

YOUTH COMMUNICATION

True Stories by Teens

FINDING MY PLACE

EXECUTIVE EDITORS
Keith Hefner and Laura Longhine

CONTRIBUTING EDITORS
Hope Vanderberg, Andrea Estepa, Sean Chambers,
Clarence Haynes, Marie Glancy, Rachel Blustain,
Duffie Cohen, Nora McCarthy, and Tamar Rothenberg

LAYOUT & DESIGN
Efrain Reyes, Jr. and Jeff Faerber

PRODUCTION
Stephanie Liu

COVER ART
YC Art Dept.
Thanks to our cover model Gamal Jones.

For reprint information, please contact Youth Communication.

ISBN 978-1-935552-29-1

Second, Expanded Edition

Printed in the United States of America

Youth Communication ®
New York, New York
www.youthcomm.org

Catalog Item #YD26-1

Table of Contents

Beating the Odds

Sayda is inspired by her aunt, an immigrant who earned a college degree through enormous hard work and sacrifice.

Part II: Making Your Plan

My College Cloud

Kenneth is feeling anxious because he doesn't have a clue about how to pick a college, how to apply, and what to do about financial aid.

So You Want to Go to College? Get Organized!

Janill lays out the basics of applying to college.

A month-by-month calendar for applying to college.

Bookin' It for the SAT

To reach her goal of attending a competitive college, Hattie sets out to learn 250 SAT vocabulary words in 228 days.

How to Write a College Essay

> *Tips on how to approach one of the most stressful parts of the application: the dreaded personal essay.*

Choosing the Right College for You

> *Anita reviews things to think about when selecting a college, including location, size, and cost.*

What to Ask When Choosing a College

> *Latonya lists common questions that prospective college applicants should ask of students, admissions officers, and alumni.*

I Want to Go to a Historically Black College

> *Regina, an African-American student, describes why she wants to attend a black university.*

Seeing for Myself

> *Visiting college campuses gives Latonya insights into college life that she could never get by just reading books.*

Contents

Community College: A Second Chance

>   *Jordan flourishes at a community college, which he*
>   *once looked down on as only a fall-back option.*

Take Our Advice: Making the Most of Academics

Study Strategies

Minnesota Merengue

>   *Kizzy is nervous about attending an overwhelmingly*
>   *white school in Minnesota. But once on campus she*
>   *makes friends of all races.*

Take Our Advice: Dealing with Distractions

Using the Book

Introduction

It's a well-known fact that minority students enroll and graduate from college at significantly lower rates than white students. The reasons are complex. Talk to many of these students in elementary school and, without hesitation, most will say that they plan to go to college. By high school, however, things have often become more complicated.

Some students may lack role models in their family and community, people with whom they identify who can show them that college is possible. They may attend schools with few resources to help students prepare and apply for college. Or, students may attend high schools so obsessed with standardized testing that students do not learn the higher-level thinking skills required for success in college. And with ever-increasing tuition and shrinking sources of financial aid, many students simply lack the money to make it through.

The stories in this book address the academic, social, cultural, and emotional aspects of preparing for and adapting to college life from the perspectives of real teens grappling with these big questions. They also offer practical strategies for choosing, applying to, and succeeding in college.

We've divided the book into four parts: The first, "Overcoming the Barriers," considers an array of obstacles and doubts faced by minority and immigrant teens as they decide whether college is in their future. In "University of Kitchen?" Orubba Almansouri dreams of attending college, but higher education is generally frowned upon for girls in her family. Instead, they are pressured to marry, often before finishing high school.

"Sometimes I get mad that my family keeps on pushing boys to go to college, even though most of them don't have any interest, while some of us girls are ready to work for it and never get a chance," Orubba writes. "Other times, I tell myself that whatever education I end up with is better than nothing."

Sayda Morales, on the other hand, tells the story of her aunt and role model, an undocumented Honduran immigrant whose family cannot afford to send her to college but who manages to get her degree in spite of numerous setbacks.

Meanwhile, Edgar Lopez writes about his internal struggle to prepare for college by developing self-discipline rather than passively depending on teachers. And Roderick Scarlett describes the financial pressures that led him to consider the army rather than college, only to realize that the military was not the right path for him. Each story emphasizes a self-reflective process, a good model for teens struggling with how to reconcile so many different—and often conflicting—needs and expectations.

The second part, "Making Your Plan," takes a close look at the college application process, guiding students step by step from choosing the right school to writing a strong admissions essay. As Kenneth Douglas confides, the idea of applying to colleges can be overwhelming, especially if you don't have a clear idea of what's expected. He writes: "As [the college cloud] approached, it flooded me with a downpour of paperwork and deadlines, and it didn't feel good. I hadn't a clue how to begin taking on this challenge—how to pick a college, how to apply, what to do about financial aid."

Kenneth's experience is common, and it sends an important message: preparing for college is a team effort. Students need to take initiative, but those around them must recognize that teens are often inhibited and uncertain about how to tap into the help they need. This section provides students, parents, and teachers practical advice about the application process, and guides them through questions about choosing the best college for them.

Of course, getting into college is only the beginning. Persevering all the way to graduation comes with its own set of academic, social, and financial challenges. In the third section, "Paying for It," teen writers provide practical advice about financial aid and tackle some of the common challenges low-income students face in financing a college education.

Finally, in "Surviving in College," we offer stories that lay out strategies for college success. From Ferentz Lafargue writing about the ups and downs of freshman year to Jordan Temple seeking a second chance in community college, the book chronicles the writers' resilience and adaptability. Sometimes, college success isn't just a question of adjusting to new expectations, but overcoming low expectations. Orlando Hawkins describes the stigma he felt starting college:

"The only thing that was going through my mind was the professor's words: He'd seen only one African-American male graduate in 15 years. In my head, those words were ringing a bell, a bell like the one that lets you know, 'Hey, it's time to go to class,' but this time it was saying, 'Hey, Mr. Hawkins, it's time for great things to happen for you, so get a move on.'"

Many students in Orlando's situation have trouble going beyond that kind of pep talk; it's difficult to sustain hope without adequate support and guidance from others. But Orlando's story shows that personal initiative can be very powerful. By making a conscious choice to resist distractions and reach out for help, Orlando discovers that college isn't just another challenge to be endured; rather, learning can be its own reward. And what you learn about yourself in the process may be the most rewarding thing of all.

In the following stories, names have been changed: *From Failure to College.*

Note to Readers

Why So Much About New York?

Some people think New York City is the center of the universe. We don't. But all of the stories in this book are by teens at Youth Communication, a New York City-based writing program, so they tend to refer to New York schools, or schools in the Northeast. Here's a little translation.

Like every state, New York has public and private colleges. One public system is called SUNY (State University of New York) and the other is called CUNY (City University of New York). Both systems have community colleges, 4-year colleges, and universities. Most states have comparable systems. For example, California has the UC (University of California) system with more than 100 community colleges, 4-year colleges, and universities. Florida, Texas, Illinois, Pennsylvania—and every other state—have similar systems. Only the names are different.

The main idea is that when you read this book, any time a writer refers to CUNY or SUNY, they are talking about a public college. Private colleges, like Columbia University or New York University, are generally much more expensive.

What About Foster Care?

Every year, about 20,000 youth "age out" of the foster care system. Too few of them go to college. Many youth in foster care participate in our writing program, and we've included a few of their stories in this book. But being in care poses special challenges (and offers some special opportunities) for college. We have a separate college book aimed just at youth in care, called *And Still I Rise*. You can order it on our website, www.youthcomm.org.

PART I:
Overcoming the Barriers

Terrence Taylor

No More Hand-Holding

By Edgar Lopez

I sat in the back of the bus next to my friend Kevin. We were on our way to Philadelphia to visit colleges with our 8th grade class, and I was happy to be away from school for the next four days. When girls sat down next to us to wait for the bathroom, I went with the old-fashioned move: the yawn and act like I'm stretching to put my arm around them. "When are we gonna go out, baby?" I asked one girl.

The main purpose of the trip was to give us a taste of college life and introduce us to college professors and students. But for us students, the real purpose was to escape from school and parents, and to have fun during the long bus rides and in the hotels. Or so I thought.

We arrived at Lincoln University in Pennsylvania, our first destination, around noon. It looked like a fun place to be.

Students were studying on the lawns and hanging out with their friends. I noticed some were still wearing pajamas, or shorts and flip-flops. I pointed out to one of my teachers that a successful educational institution did not have to require uniforms like ours did, and she just smiled and shook her head.

After lunch we went outside and gathered by some benches to listen to a group of college students speak. I was toward the back of the group, playing around with my friends and half-paying attention. "Not another boring talk," I thought.

Everything the students said, I had heard before: "College is fun but you have to balance your school life and social life," and, "All you do in college is read, so be prepared for it," and, "Buy yourself an audio recorder because college professors don't write on the board."

When my classmate Sandra (not her real name) raised her hand, I shook my head. She loved to show off her "immense" vocabulary. "What was the most perplexing experience you faced in the transition from high school to college?" she asked.

"I think having the freedom is a problem, because if you aren't serious it becomes very easy to fail," said one of the college students. That wouldn't be a problem for me, I thought. I knew how to stay focused.

"Having to buy all your materials is the hardest part because in high school, textbooks and handouts are given to you," answered a tall Hispanic student. I knew about having to purchase your own materials, so that wasn't a shock either.

My teacher's nephew Michael, an African-American freshman, was next. "The hardest thing for me was not having teachers who were close to me. I went to a small school in Manhattan like you guys, where all the teachers were supportive and gave students that extra push to succeed. They don't do that here. All they want is their tuition money," he said.

Suddenly, I was like, "Whoa." He seemed just like us—a young male from the city. That connection allowed me to see for the first time the situation I might face in a few years. And it terrified me.

My school, which I've attended since 6th grade, is small and all the students and teachers know each other well. I was a decent student but I was lazy and held my work on cruise control. My teachers often pushed me to do better and offered a lot of extra help. I'd grown accustomed to that nurturing and expected it to continue as I got older.

Hearing how different college would be from someone with an experience similar to mine made me scared I might be unsuccessful there. I didn't know how to get things done without that extra push from teachers. I looked around and saw no one else moved by his words. Was I the only one who got the message?

Three days later, the long bus ride home to Brooklyn gave me a chance to reflect on my fear. I decided I needed to start working more independently now, so that by the time college came around, I'd be ready. But who was going to help me get to a point of self-reliance? Because ironically, I knew I could not become self-reliant alone. I felt I needed to slowly experience independence and grow accustomed to it.

I decided to go to the root of the problem, which was my dependence on a substitute teacher in our school, Ms. Stevenson. She was a good teacher and students could talk to her about anything. She felt we all had great potential and she often stayed after school to give us extra help. I decided I had to ask her if she could help me become more independent.

Two days after we returned from the trip, I nervously walked down the stairs toward Ms. Stevenson's office. I didn't want my request to backfire and have one of my most supportive teachers no longer be there for me. Or, even worse, she might think I was ungrateful for all her help.

"Ms. Stevenson, may I please speak to you?" I said, standing in the doorway of her office.

"Sure Edgar, what's wrong?" she said. She must have figured it was important because I wasn't known to miss lunch over a conversation.

I started out by telling her what the college students had told us on the trip. Then I told her, "Ms. Stevenson, I need to learn how to approach problems with my schoolwork on my own. I really appreciate all the help you give me, but if I don't get used to doing stuff on my own now, by the time college comes around I'm going to be in trouble," I said.

I was relieved when she said, "I understand and I'm glad you've decided to do this." Later that day, we met and made a plan.

Her first idea was to stop checking on me. Ms. Stevenson would often come by my class and give me a mad look if she saw me playing around. I knew that look meant "get to work," and I counted on it to get focused.

We agreed that if she no longer did that, it would force me to get serious on my own, for my own benefit. We also agreed that I would stop going to her for help with schoolwork unless I made an extra effort on my own first.

Hearing how different college would be from someone similar to me made me scared that I might be unsuccessful there.

It was a good plan. Unfortunately, it didn't work. Right away, I took advantage of our deal and became more of a slacker than ever. I walked around in the hallway during class because I knew Ms. Stevenson wouldn't be checking on me. I knew I wasn't achieving my goal of self-reliance, but slacking off was like an addiction. Besides, I was confident I could perform on the tests, so my grades would be fine.

Then my report card arrived in June. My average had plummeted about 10 points for the first time ever. I felt horrible. It made me feel that I couldn't do this alone, and I felt even less confident in my ability to perform in college. But I told myself that nobody just changes overnight. I had to keep trying.

"You're back," Ms. Stevenson said when I appeared in her office again.

"Yeah, have you seen my report card?" I said.

"I knew this would happen. Do you see what I've been trying to keep you away from?"

That report card turned out to be a good reality check. Now I knew what would happen if I wasn't self-reliant. I needed to get serious about becoming a more independent student.

I decided I needed to start working more independently so that by the time college came around, I'd be ready.

Over the next year, my freshman year in high school, there were many more obstacles on my path to self-reliance. I failed biology my first semester and did poorly in math.

But all the work I handed in was mine alone. It felt good that I wasn't going to Ms. Stevenson for help. After I did badly that first semester, I decided to cut out the baby in me and do what I needed to do to improve my grades.

I developed a study schedule. Every day I devoted no less than 30 minutes to every subject I received homework for, instead of not studying at all, like before. Instead of complaining that I didn't know a topic, I began to read more about it.

And instead of spending money on expensive sneakers or clothes, I invested in myself. I went to Barnes & Noble and found biology textbooks that targeted high school graduation exams and went into more depth than my schoolbooks.

By the end of my freshman year, I realized I was working independently. My study habits were now a part of my routine. My greatest moment was seeing my report card that June.

I had done better in all of my classes. I was most excited to see an 85 for my French class, the hardest class I had. Through my own persistence I had improved my grade by 15 points.

Now I never expect anyone to hold my hand and do my work for me. I'm not a machine that knows everything, but I don't automatically run for help anymore when I can't comprehend something. This has helped me prepare for the real world, during college and after it.

Edgar was 17 when he wrote this story.

Kat Morris

The Army's Not for Me

By Roderick Scarlett

About a year ago, I briefly considered joining the military because I felt I'd derailed my college plans.

Since freshman year, I had wanted to go to a prestigious private university in New York City, like New York University or Columbia. Because it's expensive to go to a "good" college like those, I planned to get plenty of scholarship money by studying hard and getting high grades. I couldn't afford those schools on my own.

At first, my plan seemed attainable. But I didn't focus on what I needed to do to reach my goals. As a sophomore and junior, I had bouts of depression and laziness, which affected my academic performance. My grades became inconsistent. One marking period I had an A average on my report card and the next I had Cs and Ds. Plus, I didn't study for my SAT test.

Although I got a decent score, it wasn't high enough for me to be a competitive applicant to NYU or Columbia.

I also didn't get involved with any extracurricular activities, like student government or the basketball team. Participating in these activities would've increased my chances of getting in to top colleges and being selected for scholarships. Even though I knew this, I still let myself fall into a pile of dog mess.

By spring semester of my junior year, I realized that I wouldn't get into a "good" school based on my school performance. So I started to search for new solutions. I considered attending a City University of New York (CUNY) or State University of New York (SUNY) school because I knew I wouldn't have to borrow much money to pay for tuition.

But many of my friends and relatives who went to CUNYs or SUNYs said it's more difficult to find a job with a degree from one of these universities, since many employers judge people by what college they attended. So I quit thinking about that option.

That's when I began to seriously consider joining the armed forces. I'd seen many military commercials on TV over the years, and usually ignored them. But one day, feeling desperate and seeing a future full of clouds, I was pulled in by a 30-second Army commercial. Those helicopters whizzing by to the "Be All That You Can Be" slogan sparked my interest.

From what I saw, the Army offered full-time recruits university tuition, college credits, jobs, and physical fitness. This sounded spectacular to me. I grew excited about joining the military because it seemed like something adventurous that could get me into a top school. I was so energized that I didn't feel worried about being in a combat situation.

But over the next week, I thought more about what combat would be like. I thought about being put into a "kill or be killed" situation. I imagined myself firing automatic weapons at men and seeing their chests explode, and their uniforms turn dark red. I actually sat down in my living room and tried to imagine what it would be like to be blown away. It was painful.

From what I've read and seen on TV, America is lavish in its use of military force. I don't think America should've dropped atomic bombs on Hiroshima and Nagasaki during WWII, or participated in the Vietnam and Persian Gulf wars. I soon realized that I couldn't fight for a country whose military philosophies I disagree with.

Feeling desperate about college and seeing a future full of clouds, I was pulled in by a 30-second Army commercial.

But then I returned to my all-too-familiar state of uncertainty about college. Near the end of junior year, in the midst of my haze, my class went to a college fair. The fair had representatives from mostly public colleges, so I began to reconsider those schools. I talked about my concerns for my future with one woman from CUNY.

"I know that CUNY schools don't charge a lot of money for tuition, but will I be able to get a good job with a degree from the university?" I asked her.

"Yes, you can," she said. She seemed honest, telling me that some employers will discriminate against a CUNY degree. But she also added that most employers will be more concerned with the experience I have in whatever career I choose rather than where I got my degree from, and that I should get some work experience as early as I can. "But you will have to work extra hard," she said.

The fact that she emphasized hard work made me feel like I could be a success, even if I don't end up at a top private university. Her words, along with advice from other representatives, convinced me to continue my education after high school without the military. Being a poor guy just means that I have to work harder.

Roderick was in high school when he wrote this story.

John Jones

University of Kitchen?

By Orubba Almansouri

"We're halfway through the summer. Are we going to New York or what?" I asked my older sister Yasmin. She had come to visit us at our house back in my country, Yemen. We were in the room we'd shared until she got married and moved away.

"Do you really want to go?" she replied, opening the Kit Kat bar she had in her hand.

"Yes and no," I answered as I lay down on my bed. "I want to stay here for you and all our extended family, but I also want to see Dad and New York City."

"What's the rush, then? It's not like you're going to school when you get there," she said.

In my family, most men believe that the best place for a woman is in the house and the best job for us women is to cook, clean and raise a family. Many girls in my family—including

Yasmin—stop going to school before high school, and none have gone to college. Girls live with their families until they are 15 or a little older, then it's time to say goodbye to being single and hello to marriage.

My religion (Islam) is not against girls being educated. In fact our Prophet Mohammed, may peace be upon him, said that we should seek education even if we have to go to China for it. The problem isn't my culture either, since many Yemeni girls are educated and have jobs. Where my family's tradition came from, I don't know. But so far, no one has broken it.

I never imagined my destiny would be any different. In my country I was an excellent student and teachers loved me. In 7th grade, I was first in my class. They put my name in big letters on a piece of paper and hung it up in the main hallway. I felt so proud of myself.

I didn't mind leaving school at any time, though, because I knew the path girls in my family followed and I didn't expect anything else. When we came to the United States the first time (when I was 5—we stayed for a few years), my older sisters were teenagers and they didn't get a chance to go to school, even though they really wanted to go and learn English. So when I was 14 years old and I heard that we were moving back to the US, I figured I wouldn't be going to school anymore.

Then we got to New York, and my dad announced he was planning to enroll my sister Lebeya and me in school. I was surprised. From what I used to see on TV, American high schools were another planet compared to schools in Yemen. I wasn't used to going to school with boys, or talking to them. In fact, I was a little worried: I'd heard that many Yemeni students who go to American high schools start to do what the other kids are doing, like having relationships and even drinking, neither of which is allowed by my religion. I'd expected my dad would want to keep my sister and me away from this environment. (My mom wants us to be educated, as she never had the chance to be, but like most Yemeni women she follows her husband's decisions.)

But my dad was determined. When my oldest sisters didn't go to school in New York, that affected their lives and his. They couldn't go out alone because they didn't understand English and couldn't communicate. My dad had to translate for them at doctors' appointments. When we moved to New York, he said putting my sister and me in school would help us become independent so we could help ourselves when necessary.

For my part, I decided that since I had the chance to go to school, I would definitely take it. Today my sisters are both married and have children sweet as honey, but they still wish they had gone to school here and learned to speak English. I saw from my sisters' experience that education was the best thing for me, and I felt that going to school might be fun and a way to get out of the house. I had no idea what it would become to me.

In my family, men believe the best place for a woman is in the house, cooking, cleaning, and raising a family.

While we were getting records and report cards sent from Yemen to New York so my sister and I could enroll here, the men in my extended family started telling my dad that we would get ourselves into trouble and hurt the family's reputation. They thought that high school in America would Americanize us, causing us to drop the traditions we'd been learning our entire lives and pick up others.

One day my dad was on the phone with one of my cousins and I heard some of my dad's replies. (It's not my fault he thought that I was sleeping when I wasn't.) They went like this:

"They are my daughters and I have raised them right. I know what is good for them."

"It's none of your business."

"I don't care what they say, I have listened to you guys once and I won't make that mistake again."

After I heard that, I was saying to myself, "Way to go, Dad!" I saw my father as someone who is ready to make a change and someone who really cares about his daughters' education; I saw him in a way that made me feel proud to be the daughter of Ali Almansouri. I knew that my dad had put all his trust in us and this made me want to be on my best behavior.

My first day at Brooklyn International High School was scary because I was starting 9th grade at the end of September and I was the new girl. I felt lonely at first, but luckily my English was OK from living here as a kid. By second period I'd talked to two Hispanic girls and we became friends. My teachers were so nice to me; they helped me when I needed help and they always asked me how I was doing. I began to love school once again. I worked hard and got excellent grades. My classmates started telling me, "You're so smart."

I don't believe that I'm as smart as they say, but I do believe that I am clever. Because I did well, ideas of actually graduating started coming into my head. My love for school grew, especially when I learned new things, went on trips or met new friends.

"You know that I will be the first girl from our family to actually go to college," I said one day to my sisters and a group of other girls, while we were sitting together talking.

"Yeah, and you'll go to the University of Kitchen," my younger cousin said.

"And earn your cooking degree," my sister added.

Then they all started laughing, including me. "You'll see when I become the first Almansouri girl to go to college and break the 'girls don't go to college' rule," I said. "You'll see what I will do."

The truth is, though, that there is always a question mark over my future. In spite of the things I overheard my dad say on the phone, his decisions about my future are not all made yet. My dad doesn't really follow up on my schoolwork, and when opportunities come up—like leadership programs, after-school activities, or writing articles like this one for Youth Communication—it's not easy to get his permission to participate.

I think that even though he put me in school, sometimes he

still thinks the way other men in my family do. This worries me, because it makes me think he may not allow me to finish the path that he let me start. However, if I give him a great speech about why he should let me do some extracurricular thing, and if I'm persistent, he usually gives in. I think that when I put it in his head that I can benefit a lot from these things, he sees it, and that gives me hope for the future.

My being allowed to finish high school and go to college depends on two people: Dad and me. I will never disobey him because he is everything to me. My basic hope is that we don't go back to Yemen before I graduate from high school. Then, if my dad lets me, I'd prefer to put off marriage until I am settled in college.

What will actually happen, I don't know. My dad hasn't told me what he's thinking. Even though I hate not knowing what's going to be next, in another way I don't want the topic to come up yet. I'm afraid of the answer I'll get, in case it's a "no." Anyway, as they say, you have to walk up the ladder step by step or you'll fall down.

When I'm feeling hopeful, I think my dad will let me go to college. I want to attend a good one like Columbia University, major in English or journalism and also study biology. I see my future as a finishing line with red and white stripes, and I see myself crossing the line, then getting my prize—in other words, working in a career and feeling true power and independence. I also want to feel useful to the world and to people around me. I want to learn more and be an educated person.

Sometimes, though, I feel that everything I do is for no reason and that I will never be able to go to college or even finish high school. I worry that if I do graduate from high school, my dad will say, "I already let you finish high school and we don't have women who go to college in this family." I worry about the pressure that will be on him if he does let me go to college. Our family made such a big deal about us going to high school, I can't imagine what they would say about college.

When I hear things like, "Look—girls your age are getting married and soon it will be your turn," those comments are like rockets landing in my ears. I find a place to be alone and think to myself, "All this hard work, these top grades, these compliments, for what? For me to remember when I'm seasoning the soup. Why did they put me in the race when I had no interest in participating? They put the idea in my head, made me like it and actually work toward something—all so that when I reach the finish line they'll tell me I can't cross it."

I imagine watching others cross the line without me, and shoot myself down for all the time I spent dreaming of things I want to accomplish. "Maybe it's not time, Orubba," I think. "Maybe the girl that will break your family's record hasn't been born yet."

I want my life to have different flavors and taste them all, not just repeat the same flavor over and over every day.

With that I cry myself to sleep. Sometimes I even have nightmares about not finishing high school. A lot of people think that it's no big deal; I'll get married and my husband will give me everything I need. But that's not enough for me because I want my life to have different flavors and taste them all, not just repeat the same flavor over and over every day. I also want to feel that I'm prepared if something happens to my husband. How will I feed my children? I want to have a weapon in my hand and education is one weapon that never hurts anyone, but actually helps.

In Yemen, I always thought that going to college was a good thing for girls, but I didn't feel envious of the girls from other families who could go. Since I came to the US, though, I have been thinking more about my future and I want more out of life. Because I see college as a possibility for me, but not a sure thing, today I feel envious toward Yemeni girls who know they can go to college.

Sometimes I get mad that my family keeps on pushing boys

to go to college, even though most of them don't have any interest, while some of us girls are ready to work for it and never get a chance. Other times, I tell myself that whatever education I end up with is better than nothing. I'm even a little afraid of going to college in case I fail. I'm torn between two things, but the tear is not straight down the middle. I'm happy that my obsession with success is greater than my worries.

Now I'm a junior, my grades are still excellent, and my desire to live my dream is greater than ever. I agree with some of my family's traditions, like girls not going out alone and not sleeping at anyone's house outside the family. But the education issue is too much. If they give all us girls a chance and support us, we can help our family reach higher than ever before. If I go to college, I'll open a path and be a role model for future generations of girls in the family, teaching them not to give up.

If my father's decision is for me to go to college, he will raise his head high and tell everyone who wanted to stand in my way that they were wrong; that he is happy and proud that he gave us a chance that a lot of parents in my family took away from their girls. I want him to be really pleased with what I accomplish.

Everything I become will be because of the trust he gave me. I will keep my religion and my traditions, but I will follow my dreams as long as I know that what I'm doing is right. I have no problem with cooking and cleaning, as long as it is a side order with my dream. But if my dad doesn't support my dream, then everything that I have planned for won't be. That's what causes me nightmares instead of dreams.

Orubba was 16 when she wrote this story.

Riona Faith O'Malley

My Sister's Courage

By Wendy Kwan

Four years ago, when my sister Katherine received an acceptance letter from a prestigious university, she was ecstatic. She had always expressed her determination to succeed in college and eventually the business world.

Unfortunately my mother did not support Katherine in her plans. My mother feared that if Katherine went to such a notable college, it would be difficult for her to find a husband because men would be intimidated by her intelligence. She knew that college meant that Katherine would be more independent and thus spend less time at home. To my mother, staying home meant staying safe, safe from real danger and safe from challenges to traditional cultural beliefs.

My mother grew up in a traditional, patriarchal (male-dominated) family in China. She was taught that men were superior to women. Because they were responsible for their families, men were considered to be stronger and more intelligent. Since a woman's goal was to marry a man, however, it was not necessary for her to be too successful or intelligent.

Even after my mother emigrated to the United States and became a working mother, she held on to this traditional idea of a woman's place. Both my sister and I tried to challenge her, but Katherine was brave enough to actually act according to her beliefs.

My mother feared that if Katherine went to such a notable college, it would be difficult for her to find a husband.

After my mother explained her fears, Katherine stared into her bewildered eyes with her own eyes flaring, her cheeks burning red and her lips pressed tightly together. "I don't believe I'm hearing this!" she said in an anguished tone. "A woman doesn't have to be a man's wife to be an important person in society. Females have become executives of companies, leaders, Supreme Court Justices...I want my chance. I beg you to give it to me."

My mother thought about what Katherine had said for many days. As a deadline for a decision came near, she reluctantly consented to my sister's attending college.

Katherine's courage began to change my mother's concept of a woman's place. It has been four years since this incident occurred and my sister will be the first one in my family to graduate from college. After graduation, she will be entering a financial management program for a distinguished company.

Katherine is truly a positive role model who has inspired me. She has a strong sense of herself; she speaks with confidence and is able to influence others with her inspirational words. When I see my sister, I see an independent, determined, and nurturing woman who has influenced my life greatly.

Wendy was a student at Barnard College when she wrote this story.

Odessa Straub

From Failure to College

By Tanisia Morris

When I was in elementary school, I dreaded parent-teacher conferences. "Welcome, it's so good to have you here," my teacher would say to my parents. I'd wish this happy tone would last forever, but the conversation always took a solemn turn, and I was the subject.

"Tanisia's a wonderful student. She tries hard. But she's still not where she needs to be for her grade level," my teacher would say. Then she'd show them my report card.

"Does she have any 3's?" my mom would ask hopefully. (Three was the highest and one was the lowest.)

"No, but she could get them if she worked hard, right, Tanisia?" my teacher would say.

I wouldn't reply. Her optimism seemed rehearsed. It felt like a mockery, because I'd failed so many times.

School had always been a problem for me. My parents spoke Jamaican English, or patois, at home. I couldn't pronounce certain words, and I often put words together differently than American English. Teachers referred to my speech as "broken English," like it was something that needed to be repaired. My self-esteem plummeted, and by 3rd grade, I just assumed I'd never be smart.

Still, I wanted so badly to know how it felt to be successful at something. By 5th grade, I desperately wanted to make a fresh start, but I didn't know how. My parents tried to help me, but they became frustrated when they'd go over the work with me and I still couldn't get it.

Then, a couple weeks before starting junior high, I called my grandmother in Jamaica. She noticed that I was quieter than usual. "How's everything?" she asked.

"Oh, everything's just fine," I said, trying to convince her when I couldn't even convince myself. Finally, I told her about my fear of failing in school again.

I started experimenting with different learning methods to find out what was best for me.

"You're going to achieve so much," she said with conviction. "I know you're going to make it. Trust me, you can do anything you want as long as you're determined."

I was quiet for a moment. I wanted to say, "But Grandma, I failed. My report card will make you think differently." But she continued speaking.

"I know you're going to make me proud," she said. She reminded me that no one in my family had gone beyond high school and she knew I'd be the one to break the mold. For the first time, I felt hopeful. Someone believed in me, and I didn't want to disappoint her.

At the beginning of 6th grade, keeping her words of encouragement in mind, I started experimenting with different learning methods to find out what was best for me. Soon I realized that it's not just "smarts" but study habits and determination that lead to success.

In science class, I had to memorize the parts of an animal cell. I found I learned best by drawing diagrams. I studied a diagram about the cell's structure in my textbook and then I drew the cell on my own without the labels. I examined my picture until I could visualize and remember the parts that made the cell whole, and I could label the parts and their functions without looking at the textbook.

I realized that asking questions made me less confused and helped my teacher understand the way I thought.

In math class, I began to review math problems with my teacher. In the past, I'd seldom asked my teachers for help because I didn't want them to think I wasn't smart enough do it on my own. Now I realized that asking questions made me less confused and helped my teacher understand the way I thought, so that she could learn to explain problems in ways I could understand.

I also took advantage of my school's tutoring programs in math and reading. Two days a week, I worked with a group of students and a math teacher for about three hours. At home, I followed up with practice exercises. The other two days, we'd work on reading and writing with an English teacher. When I had the day off from my after-school programs, I'd study my notes.

In all my classes, I tried to develop better verbal and listening skills. I listened more carefully to my teachers in class, taking notes and repeating definitions and theories out loud to myself at home.

Finally, I tried learning by organizing the information in each chapter of my textbooks into outlines. It forced me to read all the text thoroughly until I had no further questions or uncertainty about the meaning. Before I knew it, I was using this method in math, science and other subjects. I started to love reading so much that I read outside of school.

I made several trips a week to the public library, often borrowing more books than I could carry. I developed a pattern of reading every day for at least two hours. I'd walk up to the second floor of the library and put my book bag down at the last table near the history books.

Surrounded by hundreds of books, I felt like a kid in a candy store, and once I chose a book, I hardly ever made it back to my seat. I'd sit on the floor with my eyes buried in the pages. I liked the burning sensation I felt when I kept my eyes on the page too long.

Within a couple months, my test grades were higher and I was above many of my classmates. Teachers complimented me on my work. Some of my classmates thought I worked hard because I was a suck-up or I feared disappointing the teacher. But my only fear was disappointing my grandmother, the person who believed in me.

She kept me motivated all through junior high and high school. My parents noticed my progress and began encouraging me to keep up the good work. And during my junior year of high school, it all paid off. The head of the history department asked me to take a college-level class, Advanced Placement U.S. History and Government, with 12 other students.

I tried learning by organizing the information in each chapter of my textbooks into outlines.

At first I wasn't sure I could handle college level work. But I kept remembering my grandmother's advice: "…you can do anything you want as long as you're determined." It was the alarm clock I needed to wake me up whenever I doubted my abilities.

The classes were demanding. We had to read about 40 pages a night from our advanced level textbook, and my government teacher didn't accept the simple answers so many of us were accustomed to giving.

"What is the main job of the judicial system?" he asked the

class one day. Most of us raised our hands, so sure we knew the correct answer.

"The judicial system's job is to interpret the Constitution," I said, as my other classmates nodded in agreement.

"You're 100%—"

"Right!" I thought to myself.

"Wrong," he said. "The judicial system settles disputes and uses the Constitution as a reference."

Getting the wrong answer felt different from the criticism I'd experienced as a child. I didn't feel foolish because I knew the teacher saw my potential. He constantly challenged me to improve my thinking.

My only fear was disappointing my grandmother, the person who believed in me.

It was in that class that I began developing a connection with other students who shared my drive to succeed. One day the class took a field trip to the Tenement Museum in Manhattan. Afterwards we all went to a pizza shop in Little Italy and talked about our future plans. College was on everyone's priority list, which was a breath of fresh air compared to most of my other classmates in school.

"I want to go to Columbia University," Carlita said. "I've been taking extra classes to meet their requirements."

"I want to own my own clothing line and eventually have a franchise," Katie said.

"That's good, but that industry's really competitive," one of my other classmates said. "It might take you a long time to get to that dream."

I expected Katie to lose some hope after this remark. But she replied, "I don't expect it to come easily, but I'm creative. I know I'm going to make it."

Her words brought me back to that day when my grandmother told me I was going to succeed. I realized my classmates must have also had moments in their lives when they doubted themselves. But, like me, they'd somehow managed to dismiss negativity from others and believe in themselves. Then it hit me that I was now one of them—one of the "smart kids." I'd finally achieved the goal I'd had since elementary school.

Now I'm halfway through my freshman year at Lehman College, and excelling in all my classes. In elementary school, college seemed a dream that many thought I'd never achieve. I'm so glad I refused to give in to other people's perceptions of the person I could become.

My grandmother tells me she knew it all along. She still encourages me and never fails to tell me how proud she is of me, each time we talk on the phone. And once my parents saw my potential, they never doubted my abilities.

Although they couldn't help me as much as I needed, they taught me a very important lesson in the process: independence. I learned that, in the end, I was the only one who could change my pattern from failure to success.

Tanisia was 19 when she wrote this story.
She later graduated from Lehman College.

Are You the First in Your Family to Go to College?

I am. My mom was like, "Do not mess up. The hopes of your family are riding on it."

Tasha Santos, 20

My parents went to school in Trinidad but here it's a whole new system. My brother went before me and he had to figure everything out. I remember there were a lot of arguments between him and my parents. I think when you're the first in your family to go through the system, you have to take the initiative and talk to officials and find out what's going on, because you really don't know the whole bureaucracy of college.

Desiree Bailey, 19

Janill Briones, 21

In my immediate family I'm the first one. I know my parents are really proud of me and that makes me happy. They both grew up in Ecuador. My dad only made it to 3rd grade because he had to work and my mom only made it to 6th grade because she had to take care of her brothers and sisters. So they always wanted me to do well in school. I do it mostly for myself, of course, but I would like to do it for them, too.

Sayda and her aunt

Beating the Odds

By Sayda Morales

"Do your homework!" she said.

"But it's boring and it's Saturday," I replied. It seemed like we always went through this argument.

"You want to go to a good college and get a good job, right? You need to start in 3rd grade," she insisted.

I'm glad my aunt, Sayda Dubok, whom my mom named me after, always pushed me to do my homework. If she hadn't, I probably wouldn't be attending the private high school I am today.

My aunt has always been a good role model to me. She was a low-income immigrant and the first in our family to attend college. She graduated with her bachelor's degree and is now 27 and has a good job at an insurance company. Her experiences inspire me to continue emulating her in all that I do. Here, in her own words, is her story:

"When I was younger, college was a difficult thing to think about. As an immigrant, my first thought was that I wasn't going to be able to afford college. I came to this country in 1994 when I was 13, after growing up in Honduras and then Mexico.

It was a long transition. I had to learn English and the way of teaching in this country. I sat in the corner listening to classmates make fun of the way I was trying to speak English. That prevented me from learning.

But in high school I became more involved. I joined the swimming team and became captain. I joined a Spanish literature group and the drama club. Those things allowed me to learn better, participate more, be more outspoken. My average went from a 65 to a 90 by sophomore year.

My friends also influenced me a lot. There was a Mexican girl who was an immigrant, too. She knew, the same as I did, that after graduating high school it was going to be pretty much the end since we couldn't afford college, at least that's what we thought. So, we were trying to get the best we could out of high school. Another friend was very smart. She went to Cornell University. All of us were on the swim team together and were competitive with each other, comparing grades.

Most of my classmates were applying to college, but I was in the U.S. illegally and my mother didn't have the money.

It wasn't always easy to compare myself to my friends, though. Senior year, most of my classmates were applying to college and I wasn't, because I was in the U.S. illegally and my mother didn't have the money for college. Through my swimming coach I did find many swim scholarships. But I didn't qualify due to my illegal status.

So instead of college, when I graduated from high school, I went to work in a café near Wall Street in Manhattan. It was during this time that I realized how important education was.

A lot of customers made me feel like the only thing I knew how to do was serve coffee. I used to cry sometimes at night because I felt I could do a lot better. I had many friends who had gone straight to college and I was jealous. I'm a competitive person and I felt like I was staying behind. I missed going to school, learning and growing intellectually.

Then I remembered how when I first came to the U.S., my mother took me to her job as a housekeeper. I saw her cleaning the toilet and she told me, "You see what I'm doing over here? I don't want you and your sisters to do the same thing. If I've made all these sacrifices, it has to be for something."

My mom already had five daughters and she didn't have the opportunity to go back to school. But I did. That's when I promised myself that no matter what, I was going to college.

I started part-time at Borough of Manhattan Community College, which was cheaper than a four-year college, so I managed to save enough money from my job to pay for it.

When I started college, I had been out of school for two years and I hadn't been practicing my English enough. So I had to take and retake a lot of remedial courses and spend most of my savings on that.

I continued to work as a cashier almost 11 hours a day, getting paid $4 an hour. I got up around 4 a.m. for work, and went to school afterwards. I would come home around 10 or 11 p.m., do my homework and wake up at 4 again the next day. There were times when I doubted I was going to make it because I was so exhausted. I couldn't concentrate. I wanted to exchange more with my classmates but there was no time.

But there was something that was always telling me deep inside, "You can do it!" And my four sisters were behind me because I was the only one of us in college. I felt I could be an example for them and for my nieces in the future. So I tried not to think about how tired I was. I tried not to think about the process, but to just do it. I told myself that the ends would justify the sacrifice.

After two years I switched to Baruch College, a four-year school in Manhattan, which I attended part-time as I continued to work. Luckily, by the time I ran out of money, my legal status had changed and I was able to get a better job as a typist at an auto insurance company. The owner liked me. One semester I was upset because I didn't have any money to pay for school, and he decided to lend me $1,000 and told me to pay him back when I got money from my taxes. Another time I had to ask my stepfather for a loan. Money was always a problem.

I was the only one in college. I felt I could be an example for my sisters and for my nieces.

During my last semester, I went through a difficult surgery and it was hard to concentrate. By then I was with my fiancé and he supported me financially and emotionally. That's how I managed to graduate in 2006, after five and a half years, with a BA in small business management and a minor in political science.

Since then, I've been working for the same insurance company. I've been promoted and I have a lot of responsibility, which I like, but I don't think I'll stay here long-term. I'm married now and pregnant. My plan is to take care of the baby for two years and go back to school for my master's in management during that time. Then I'd like to work for a bank. I have to think big.

Sayda was 15 when she interviewed her aunt.

PART II:
Making Your Plan

Stephanie Wilson

My College Cloud

By Kenneth Douglas

That big, dark cloud had been coming toward me for some time now. I had no clue what to do about it, and when I finally did start to reach for an umbrella, it seemed too late. But that's only because I'd never seen a cloud like it before.

That cloud was college. As it approached it flooded me with a downpour of paperwork and deadlines, and it didn't feel good. I hadn't a clue how to begin taking on this challenge—how to pick a college, how to apply, what to do about financial aid.

On top of all that, I didn't even want to go to college. I like learning. But between the agonizing application process and the idea of paying thousands of dollars to go to school, the door of opportunity seemed unreachable. So sometimes the solution seemed to be not to go at all.

But I didn't want my dream to get washed away. For my

dream job—a video game developer—or starting my own company, I need skills that I just don't have right now, like computer programming and knowing how to run a business. I need higher education for that. But what colleges might be best for my goal? And would they accept me? Could I afford it? Where could I get the information I need?

My mother isn't much help. She was born in Guyana and didn't go to college, or to an American high school. In Guyana, many people only go to school until they're 16. Then they go to a trade school or start working, or if they pass an exam, go to senior secondary school. My grandmother has plenty of advice. She constantly tells me I need to

I hadn't a clue how to begin—how to pick a college, how to apply, what to do about financial aid.

learn to fix fridges and heaters, so I can make a lot of money. But I don't have any kind of fixing talent and don't care to develop any.

My brother, Kevin, is in college at Florida A&M University (FAMU). But we don't get along. So I don't listen to his advice, which consists of tips like, "Look for a school in a climate you like," and "Make sure there are enough dorms."

My high school hasn't given me the help I've sought either. It's had a few college-based events, but no one there ever sat down with me and said, "OK, this is what you'll need to know for college, and this is what they'll expect from you." What they have done is hand out letters congratulating us on becoming seniors, and telling us how it's our and our parents' responsibility to get us into a college.

My school used to throw a college fair each year. But they really should've called it a "college circus." There were dozens of booths set up, everyone showing something flashy to get your attention.

Offers were just flying at you left and right: "Step right up, come and get your Ivy League! Hurry, hurry, hurry, we're almost out of small, personal campuses!" It even had that carney smell.

But maybe that's just because it was held in the gym.

I remember how even in a gym filled with people I felt alone, because it all seemed so foreign to me. That was in 10th grade. Last year, in 11th grade, when I should've begun college consideration, none of my classes were scheduled to go to the college circus. And this year we didn't even have one.

But this September my school established the College Advisory Team (CAT), made up of two teacher-advisers and three counselors. CAT's mission is to "give all students [seniors] the opportunity to get into college," according to Mr. Ellis, one of the advisers.

While their efforts are sound (they make time for personal meetings with seniors and keep profiles on us), they aren't much of a team yet. I've had to fill out the same form four times for three of them (twice for the same adviser) and when the fifth time came I asked one of them, "Does CAT just not share information? I've filled this out so many times." The adviser said, "Oh, then don't worry. It must be a miscommunication."

My experience with CAT started back in September. Mr. McBeth, a CAT adviser, spoke to the senior class during the first senior meeting of the year. He explained that he was the new college adviser responsible for getting us into college for as little money out of our pockets as possible. This sounded appealing, so I went to his office. I already had a school in mind but I asked him about other schools with good computer science programs that might be able to offer me a scholarship.

But as soon as he found out my average, he just said, "All right, you're on my FAMU list," since with my grades he could probably get me in for free. Getting students into school for free seems to be his only concern–which is fine, but what I was looking for was a school geared toward my interests.

In October, I asked Mr. Ellis about CAT. He said he was glad I came to him, but that I'd already been assigned a CAT adviser named Ms. Monuma. "What?" I asked. I hadn't heard anything from Ms. Monuma. In fact, I hadn't even heard of her.

Mr. Ellis said I could talk to him about college instead. By then, I had my mind set on going to the State University of New New York (SUNY) Morrisville, which has a strong focus on computer and information sciences.

But when I asked Ellis what I needed to do to get there, he pulled out a paper that listed SUNY schools from most highly-regarded to least. He pointed to SUNY Buffalo, a school higher up than Morrisville, and suggested I go there. But again, that wasn't the help I asked for.

My entire CAT experience made me less confident about getting into the school I wanted. I'd wanted an adviser to sit me down and explain what steps I needed to take to reach my goal, not what steps to take to reach their goal for me.

I see college as a bridge from here to my future.

What little help I did feel I got at school came from the oddest places, like my statistics class. Since the teacher, Mr. Grisset, is also a respected dean, the seniors in the class would turn to him for college advice. They'd walk into class and ask stuff like, "Yo G, what about those fraternities? You think they're worth joining?" and G would begin a nostalgia-filled story (that incidentally would take up the rest of the period) about friends he'd had who were in frats.

He also filled us in on issues like scholarships and loan programs. It was reassuring to hear his perspective on college and the different paths you can take to get there, to know that if you fail a class, or get a low SAT score, you're not automatically blacklisted by colleges. And that you can take the SAT multiple times and your highest score from each part will be what colleges care about. But it was random that he was helping us, since it wasn't his job.

I decided I'd have to take matters into my own hands. I

turned to the Internet for help, and found two websites that offer information on scholarships—CollegeBoard.com and FastWeb. com. Both sites show scholarships that apply to specific characteristics (like being talented in sports, or being of a certain religion or race). I found scholarships offered by Campbell's Soup, Microsoft, other businesses, and schools themselves.

I also checked out the websites of schools I wanted to know more about. I knew that choosing a major would help me narrow my search to schools that had what I wanted. I finally thought I'd narrowed it down to computer engineering, which is learning to build and maintain computers and networks.

But then I found that some schools broke that down even further into another three majors, and I felt lost again. I had to research those new ones on the schools' websites until I found what I wanted—to learn to write computer programs.

Now I've chosen my top three state schools, including SUNY Morrisville. They offer a major in "information technology management" which combines computer engineering and business, and I'd come out with a bachelor's degree.

As of the first week of December, I'd sent out my three applications, but my school had yet to send the colleges my transcript. So I'm still feeling anxious about this seemingly endless application process.

Some people go to college to broaden their horizons, some go because their parents make them, others go to get a fancy degree. I see college as a bridge from here to my future. I just want to cross it as quickly and easily as possible and get on with my job and my life. But with this dark cloud still in my way, and with no one to guide me through it, sometimes I feel like I'll never even find that bridge.

Kenneth graduated from high school and attended the State University of New York at Stony Brook.

Patricia Battles

So You Want to Go to College? Get Organized!

By Janill Briones

When teachers, counselors, parents, and commercials tell you that college is an important step in life, believe them. In college, we'll figure out what we want to do with our lives, meet new and fascinating people, learn new skills, and, for some of us, start living on our own.

To go to college, though, first you have to apply. Applying is simple. Getting applications done on time is the killer. But don't worry—you just need a plan.

If you think you might be interested in a college, check out its website. Look into its departments, programs, courses, extracurricular activities and location. If you already know what you want to major in, make sure the college has a good department for it. If you don't know what you want to major in, make sure the college offers a variety of courses.

When college admissions officials are selecting students, they'll usually look at your grades, SAT scores, and class rank. They'll want to see if you've taken tough courses like AP or honors classes. Colleges also look at extracurricular activities, letters of recommendation, and your essays if they're required.

What's your chance of getting into a college you're interested in? You can try to figure that out by looking up the average test scores and class rank of this year's freshman class (the students they admitted last year). If the numbers you see look more or less like your own, you have a reasonable chance.

As you size up your chances of getting into colleges, sort them into three categories. First, there are your fallback or "safety" colleges, the ones you think you'd get into for sure. Next are your match or "good chance" colleges, which tend to accept students with grades, class rank, and SAT scores like yours.

Getting applications done on time is the killer. But don't worry—you just need a plan.

Finally, choose a shoot-for-the-moon college or two, places you don't think you'll get into, but you'd like to go if you could. It's worth a shot—maybe you don't have great SAT scores but have a skill or talent they'd like to have.

And don't automatically dismiss a college because it's too expensive. There's always financial aid. If you'd really like to go there, apply. Once you get in, you'll find out how much money they'll offer you.

Keep in mind that there are three types of deadlines: early decision, early action, and the regular deadline. An early decision application is binding: if you apply to a school early decision and they accept you, you have to go to that school. You can only apply early decision to one school.

An early action application doesn't bind you to the school, but it allows you to know sooner if you were accepted or not.

These early deadlines are usually around November.

Going for the regular deadline (usually around January) will give you more time to apply, and it will give you the chance to change your mind about your first choice college.

If you apply to private colleges, you may be called in for an interview. Again, be yourself, but a more dressed-up version of yourself. Make sure you know something about the school before you go for the interview and come prepared with some questions of your own. If they don't ask you for an interview, ask them for one.

---

*Janill attended the City University of New York
at Hunter College.*

College Application Timeline

By Janill Briones

If you're in high school and thinking about college, this calendar can help you plan.

JUNIOR YEAR: FALL SEMESTER

• Sign up for and take the PSAT.

• Start thinking about which colleges you might want to apply to. A meeting with your school guidance or college counselor can help you figure out where to start.

SPRING SEMESTER

• Ask your counselor about free or low-cost SAT prep classes, and take one if you can.

• Sign up for and take the SAT.

• Call any colleges in your area that you might be interested in, and ask about taking a tour of the campus.

• Take advantage of any college tours offered by your school or other organizations.

SUMMER

• Make a list of schools you want to apply to. Research them at www.collegeboard.com or in college books at the library.

SENIOR YEAR: SEPTEMBER

• Research colleges if you haven't already done so. Look for college guides in the library and check out university websites.

• Get started on your applications if you plan to apply for early decision or early action.

• Update your resume.

• Make an appointment to see your college counselor.

• Register to take the SAT (or SAT Subject Tests) in October or November.

OCTOBER

• Start asking your teachers, coaches and counselors who know you well for letters of recommendation.

• Take the SAT (or SAT Subject Tests) or register to take the December SAT (or SAT Subject Tests).

• Search for grants and scholarships.

NOVEMBER

• Get your essays proofread and give your proofreader plenty of advance notice.

• Make sure teachers send out letters of recommendation on time.

• Here's another chance to take the SAT or SAT Subject Test.

DECEMBER

• Finish applying to all of your choice colleges before winter break.

• Here's another chance to take the SAT or an SAT Subject Test.

JANUARY

• Fill out your Free Application for Federal Student Aid (FAFSA).

• Have your counselor send your mid-year grade report to the colleges that require them.

• Search for more grants and scholarships.

FEBRUARY

• Contact the colleges you applied to and make sure they received all of the application materials if you haven't heard from them yet.

• Fill out your state's tuition assistance program application (check to make sure your state doesn't have an earlier deadline).

MARCH

• Search for more grants and scholarships.

APRIL

• You'll have received most of the college responses by now, so consider everything there is to know about each college and make your decision.

• Tell the colleges you aren't going to attend that you've turned them down.

MAY

• If you take any AP exams, make sure your scores are sent to your college.

JUNE

• Have your counselor send your final transcript to your college.

• Sign up for freshman orientation!

Helpful Resources

Books:

- The College Board's College Handbook

- Fiske Guide to Colleges

- Peterson's Four-Year Colleges

- The Princeton Review's The Best 357 Colleges

Websites:

- The College Board (www.collegeboard.com) covers colleges and universities throughout the country.

- College Confidential (www.collegeconfidential.com) has a national focus and lots of articles and discussions about choosing a college.

- CollegeView (www.collegeview.com) covers schools throughout the country and includes a special section on historically black colleges and universities (HBCUs).

• The Princeton Review (www.princetonreview.com) surveys students to rank schools in categories like "Diverse Student Population," "Professors Get High Marks," and "Dorms Like Dungeons."

• National College Access Network (www.collegeaccess. org) Need a pre-college plan and supportive advisers? A college access program near you is as easy as typing in your zip code.

• Know How 2 Go (www.knowhow2go.org) This site breaks down the college preparation process by grade level for high school students.

• Council for Opportunity in Education (www.coenet. us) Here you can find out about excellent programs like Upward Bound and Talent Search, which are funded by the federal government to help low-income middle and high school students get ready for college.

Leo Maisouradze

Bookin' It for the SAT

By Hattie Rice

Over the summer, I decided that I was going to study a little bit every week for the SAT. I was thinking about my long-term goal, which is to attend a competitive four-year college. I figured out a **coherent** plan and did some calculations. To master the most frequently used words on the SAT by December, I'd have to learn 250 words in 228 days. Maybe you're thinking, "Damn, that's a lot of words," but I'd be damned if all my traveling from my group home in the Bronx to the library in Queens (I don't like the loud libraries in the Bronx) was going to be wasted.

My goal is to get a score halfway between the average scores for Harvard and UCLA (University of California, Los Angeles). Perhaps you're thinking, "You talk a good one, but how you plan on doing that?" Well, the answer is very simple: by studying my trusty Princeton Review for the SAT—the next best thing to cheating.

The book is **didactic**, telling you the do's and don'ts of choosing an answer. (Thank the Lord, the SAT is mostly multiple choice.) The book has sections on the math techniques used on the test, the 250 most common SAT vocabulary words, and three practice tests so you can get a sense of how to take the test and what your real score might be. Sounds simple, right?

My first week, I found studying kind of hard because SAT words are so boring. I defined each word, wrote it three times, and used it in a sentence. I also spent a couple of minutes looking at the math techniques. Yup, extremely borringo. (Like my Spanglish?)

But I kept studying, because I knew that getting a good SAT score would be an **investment** in my future. I needed these words to succeed in college and to communicate in the corporate world.

The hardest part of studying is being mentally ready to do it. You have to make studying a priority even when you don't feel like it. A few bad situations gave me the **impetus** and drive to stay focused. First, I was often called "retarded" and "slow" by students and teachers when I was little, because I did not participate in class. I dropped out of school for most of a year, partly because I hated school and partly because I felt I needed to take care of my mom, who has mental health problems.

I set a goal of using at least one SAT word in conversation during the day.

When I came into foster care a few years ago, I found that I'm actually good at school. (I have a 90 average this semester!) Now my grades **substantiate** that I'm **incontrovertibly** smart. The kids who still think I'm not that bright will think twice when I get into the college of my dreams.

Another bad situation is my group home, where it's more popular to chill in the streets than keep your nose in the books. Luckily, the more **contemptuous** I feel towards the girls in my group home, the better my study habits. Feeling like an outcast fuels me to study. Studying is my personal **vendetta**—I will show these people that the tension and negative energy in the house will not hold me back. I deal with my rage by pushing myself to meet my goals.

T he greatest barrier to studying is that it's hard to concentrate when you have painful, pressing matters on your mind. My family is dealing with serious problems. My mother suddenly doesn't recognize anyone in the family. My father lost his job and my parents got evicted from their apartment. I'm worried about them, but I tell myself, "There's nothing you can do."

I hope that by achieving a good SAT score I'll be one step closer to graduating from college, earning a high salary, living on my own, and providing my mother and father with the help they need. I can only hope my plan will run **fluidly** because I'm very systematic and have basically planned my whole life. Plus, I'm very strong-minded (that's my way of saying stubborn). The only support I feel I need is from my bra.

To keep myself on task throughout the summer, I made sure I completed my SAT studying before doing anything fun. I also set a goal of using at least one SAT word in a conversation I had during the day.

After two months, I decided to take a practice test. I've never felt so remedial as when I saw the results. Expanding my vocabulary and thinking beyond the box are two of my finest qualities, but this test made me feel like a jackass. I got maybe three out of 10 right. My score **petrified** me. It seemed that I might fail in my quest to attend a good college and had studied all those hard words for nothing.

For a few days, my practice test score left me shaken. I felt scared of failing and suddenly doubted my intelligence. I wondered whether I would ever be ready for the SAT. What if my best was not enough? What if I couldn't achieve my goal?

Then I changed my perspective. I realized my score was just

an indication that I could not be **lenient** with myself. I would have to commit myself to the task of learning these words, even though doing so will consume a lot of my time. I have to view myself as a wounded soldier fighting for her pride.

No matter what my score is, my biggest accomplishment may be that I've made myself follow rules even when I don't like what I have to do. I think it's great that I have so much discipline. It's a triumph that I've tried my best to excel no matter what **disconcerting** situations stand in my way. I hope I've set a **precedent** for my future. Living right next door to the projects and going to one of the most dangerous schools in New York City, I'm constantly reminded of what my future might look like if I don't go to college to escape.

No matter how well I do on the SAT, my score will be better than it would've been without studying.

Ultimately, while reaching my goal has been more difficult than I had imagined, studying has been **salutary**. When I returned to school in the fall, I used my SAT words in essays and used my study skills to prepare for tests, and my grades improved.

I know studying will help me way more than chilling on the streets. No matter how well I do on the SAT, my score will be better than it would've been without studying. My goal will be tough to reach, but I believe in reaching for the moon. If I miss, I'll be among the stars.

Hattie was 17 when she wrote this story. She graduated from high school and went to college in upstate New York.

Improve Your SAT Vocabulary

Did you notice the SAT words in Hattie's story?
Here's what they mean—happy studying!

Coherent: Logically connected, makes sense

Didactic: Instructive

Investment: A contribution you make in hopes of a big return

Impetus: A motivating force or impulse

Substantiate: Verify something with proof

Incontrovertibly: Indisputable, definitely

Contemptuous: Scornful

Vendetta: A long feud or fight to get back at someone

Fluidly: Easily flowing

Petrified: Extremely scared

Lenient: Easy on, tolerant

Disconcerting: Upsetting, surprising

Precedent: A previous situation you can use as a guide

Salutary: Beneficial

Marcus Pierno

How to Write a College Essay

By Esther Rajavelu

Imagine sitting at your table and wondering what to write about yourself to impress someone you've never even met. Add to that the stress of feeling like the rest of your life may depend on what you write. For many people, that's what the experience of doing an essay for their college applications is like.

Personal essays are a required part of applications for most private colleges, and some public colleges. Some schools give you a specific question to answer while others tell you to write about anything you want. But all of them want you to use the essay to tell them something about yourself that they won't find anywhere else on your application.

"The important thing to keep in mind is that the most difficult task an admissions officer has is looking at a folder full of papers and trying to figure out who is behind the papers. That's where the essay comes in," said Ed Custard, a former college admissions officer and author of The Big Book of Colleges.

Helena Ku, a college and employment counselor, agreed. "They've seen the numbers—your grade point average, SATs— and they want to get to know the person behind the numbers, what you think and feel," she said.

For Jennifer Fondiller, a college admissions director, the essay serves two main purposes. "One is to see the ideas and thoughts that you have. Your personal background and upbringing and also the thoughts you have about the world around you," she said. "The other is to see your writing ability."

How important a factor the essay is in determining whether or not you're accepted "varies from college to college," Fondiller said. (It's "very important" at her college, she said.) As a general rule, community colleges and many state colleges do not require essays. But a really good essay can tip the scales in your favor at a selective college if you're on the borderline, according to Custard. If your grades aren't high enough, the essay gives you a chance to highlight other things you have going for

Use the essay to tell the admissions staff something about yourself that they won't find anywhere else on your application.

you—personal qualities or special talents. And, Custard added, "strong writing always has a positive effect."

Fondiller agreed. "I do see students who write well, but don't do well in school," she said. "We then look at the teacher's recommendations, etc."

For many students, the hardest part of the essay is deciding what to write about. That's why Fondiller's advice is to start thinking about it as early as possible, especially if you plan to apply to competitive schools. "The summer of your junior year is a good time to start. It might take you three months to figure out a topic," she said.

Ku agreed. "Give yourself enough time to think about what

you want to write because that process might take longer than the actual writing," she said.

*I*f you think the way to impress admissions officers is by writing about an "important" topic like nuclear energy or world peace, you're wrong. Write "what you feel comfortable writing about," said Ku. "Not what you think the admissions officer wants to hear, but what you want to write."

Everyone I interviewed agreed that it's best to write about your own life. "I would encourage everyone to write a personal essay," Custard said. "Why would you choose to give up the opportunity to show the admissions officers why you are an attractive student?"

Fondiller agreed. "You shouldn't pick something you are not personally connected with or an entirely new topic to you. Just pick a slice of your life," she said.

For example, Fondiller said that when she was applying to colleges, "I lived in a town that was far from my high school, and I had a long commute. I wrote my essay on everything I thought about every day on my way, the people I met and how it really shaped my life," she said.

You should write about something that will "make you stand out in the crowd," as Ku put it. That's why Custard thinks it's best to avoid topics like "How My Coach Changed My Life" or "My Trip to Spain." "They are too common," he said.

Writing about a negative experience can work if it had a positive effect on you in the long run. "What you want to focus on [with negative topics] are the lessons you've learned and how that experience affected you or might affect you in the future," Fondiller said.

Even though the main purpose of the essay is to help the admissions officers get to know you, they also look at how well you write. "If it's good ideas without good organization, then it's not as attractive," Fondiller said.

It's also important to get feedback on the content of your

essay. It's not cheating to show it to a family member or a teacher to see what they think. But remember that you're supposed to write about something that's important to you, not something that's important to your mother. "Consider the [feedback] of the source, but ultimately be true to yourself," Custard said.

When you're done, have someone proofread the final version to make sure there are no spelling or grammar mistakes. You don't want something as small as a spelling or grammar error to affect your chances of getting in. But don't give the essay to your reader the day before the application is due. They'll need time to do a thoughtful and thorough read, and you'll need time to make changes.

And, although it may seem as if your whole future depends on it, you'll write a better essay if you relax a little. "Don't make the writing an ordeal," Custard said. Fondiller agreed. "Just write from your heart," she said.

Esther went on to attend Wesleyan University and the Wharton School of Business.

Karolina Zaniesienko

Choosing the Right College for You

By Anita Chikkatur

Deciding which colleges to apply to isn't just about figuring out "Where can I get in?" It's also about finding a place where you want to spend four years of your life. Not everybody is going to be happy at Yale or Harvard, even if they could get in. You might be better off at a school that's less well known if it has the kind of programs and atmosphere you want.

The best way to start is by asking yourself a few things about what kind of college you want to attend. One major factor is where you want to live for the next four years. Do you want to stay close to your hometown or are you dying to get out? Would you like to live in a city or do you feel like spending the next four years of your life on a cornfield in the middle of Iowa? Weather might be a factor; going to a school in Maine might not be a great idea if you hate cold weather. And don't forget that if you go to college away from home, there will be additional costs for room and board and transportation.

In narrowing down my own college choices, location was a huge factor. Almost all the schools I'm applying to are in the Northeast, mostly because I knew about many colleges in the area and it made my search easier.

Make sure that the colleges you're interested in offer the degree you want.

I chose not to apply to any colleges in New York City, where I live. (My parents weren't too thrilled about this.) I want a change of scenery and, for me, half of the thrill of going to college is living away from home. I'm ready to be independent, to live with people my own age, and, yes, even to do my own laundry. If I went to a school in the city, even if I lived on campus, I would be too tempted to go home every weekend with a laundry bag for my mom.

The next thing I looked at was the size of the college. I'm not really a fan of huge schools, so most of the colleges I picked have less than 5,000 students. After going to a pretty big high school, I liked the fact that small schools usually mean more personal attention and easier access to faculty. But big schools have benefits too—more people to meet, a wider variety of courses, and more extracurricular activities. And if you are into Greek life (fraternities and sororities), you'll probably have more choices at a bigger school.

In addition to looking at the total number of students, consider class size, too. Try to find out the size of a typical introductory class (such as first year biology or psychology) and who usually teaches the classes (the professors or graduate students). If you get a chance to visit a college, try to sit in on a class and to see what it's like.

Earlier this year, I visited my brother at the University of Rochester and went to an introductory course in biology with about 300 students. It was held in an auditorium and the professor had to use a microphone to make himself heard. But it wasn't as bad as I expected. The professor made it fun by asking the students a lot of questions, game show style. So even if a class is big, a good professor can make it a great experience. And besides, if the professor is really boring and the class is small, it will be harder to fall asleep without getting caught!

Speaking of classes, another criteria for choosing a college are the majors the school offers. If you think you want to major in journalism or accounting, make sure that the colleges you're interested in offer that degree.

Don't forget about your life outside of the classroom, either. If you're involved in extracurricular activities that are important to you, make sure you'll be able to continue pursuing those interests. If you're an athlete, find out about the sports teams; if you play an instrument, ask about the band or orchestra.

You don't have to rule out all colleges that seem to be too expensive, but you need to keep the price tag in mind.

Money, of course, is another big factor. Private colleges can cost more than $40,000 a year and even state and city colleges aren't exactly cheap. You don't have to rule out all colleges that seem to be too expensive, but you need to keep the price tag in mind. Ask the school about its financial aid policies. Look for private scholarships, and make sure you apply for federal and state aid (you can do this online at fafsa.gov). And you can always take out loans; just be careful that you're getting it from a reputable source with as low an interest rate as possible.

Finally, you should give some thought to that question of "Where can I get in?" Make sure your list includes a couple of "safeties." A safety school is a college where you are reasonably sure to get in (there's no guarantee, of course). To pick "safety" schools, you need to look at your high school grades and SAT scores and compare them to those of the students who were admitted to that school in the past. (This information is available in most college guidebooks.) It's also good to have a safety school in terms of money. Public universities are a lot less expensive than private ones.

On the other side, it's also OK to have a "dream school." This is a school you would love to go to but which seems beyond your reach. Some of the students every school accepts will have much lower scores than the ones listed in the guidebooks. Your chances of getting into your dream schools may be better if you have a special talent, interest or experience outside of academics.

How many colleges should you apply to? My high school allows us to apply to seven. Ed Custard, a former college admissions officer and the author of *The Big Book of Colleges*, says that's a good number, leaving plenty of room for dream schools, good bets, and safeties. If a student applies to 10 or more colleges, Custard said, she's "just putting off the final decision." The important thing, Custard said, is that "regardless of the number, every school should be a place where you'll be happy."

Anita was 17 when she wrote this story. She went to Swarthmore College, in Pennsylvania, then got a PhD in Education from the University of Pennsylvania and became a college professor.

What to Ask When Choosing a College

By Latonya M. Pogue

These are some basic questions you'll probably want to ask about the colleges you're considering. You'll find the answers to some of these questions on the college's website, so check that first. Then, try to talk with current students as well as admissions officers or alumni representatives to answer your remaining questions.

☑ How many students are enrolled at your university?

Small (under 2,000 students), medium (2,000 to 10,000) and large (more than 10,000) schools can feel very different.

☑ What is the average SAT score and grade point average of admitted students?

Like it or not, you can get a pretty good idea of your chances for admission just by comparing your scores and grades to those who got in. If your scores are in the bottom quarter (or lower) your chances are not good, unless you bring a special quality or skill that the school wants.

☑ How do I apply for financial aid?

There are some basic things you have to do for every school, like complete the FAFSA. But after that, every school and scholarship is different. The more you know, the better your chances of getting aid.

☑ What does the school cost?

Every school lists its costs, but you must be sure to include every cost that will apply to you, including tuition, housing, food, books, fees, a computer, entertainment, and travel back and forth. The "hidden costs" can be larger than you think, especially when a single textbook can cost $100.

☑ What is the average class size? Will most of my classes be in a large lecture format?

Unless you go to a small college, you will likely have some large lecture classes—from 50 to 500 students. If you simply cannot function in classes like that, you need to look carefully at small (probably private) colleges.

☑ What percentage of classes are taught by teaching assistants as opposed to professors?

Colleges try to save money by having graduate students and part-time professors (called adjuncts) teach many classes. They can be great teachers, but they won't have the same level of experience and depth of knowledge that a professor does. If you're going to be paying a lot of money for a private college, you should make sure that you'll be taught primarily by real professors.

☑ What is the average number of courses a student carries per semester? What are the maximum and minimum number allowed?

At most colleges you must take (and pass) four or five classes each semester for eight semesters to graduate on time. If you don't, it will cost you. If you fail a couple classes and have to take another semester, you pay for it. If you drop a couple classes, you could lose your financial aid. (On the other hand, if you're very organized and hard-working, you may be allowed to take extra classes and graduate up to a year early.)

☑ **What are the most popular majors?**

If your main interest is English, and the most popular major is engineering, you may feel out of place. (Or you may feel special... it depends on you and on the school.) But it does make a difference in terms of the kinds of classes you have to choose from and the quality of instruction.

☑ **Do you accept Advanced Placement (AP) credit and, if so, what is the minimum score you must have on the AP exam to get credit?**

If you're counting on getting college credit for your AP classes, you must know the school's policy.

☑ **Are there opportunities to study abroad?**

Most four-year college offer this nowadays. But programs vary. If this is important to you, you will want to get details: How many students participate? What countries do they go to? Can you transfer credits if you go to a program sponsored by a different school? Etc.

☑ **Will I be guaranteed on-campus housing for all four years?**

It can be reassuring to know that there's an on-campus housing guarantee, but it's not essential. If you need private housing in your senior year, for example, you'll find it.

☑ **What academic, health and other support services exist for students?**

Colleges offer a wide range of support services nowadays, but there is a wide range of quality. The only way to really find out how good they are for someone like you is to ask around. If you think you'll need tutoring, talk to people who get it. If you occasionally suffer from depression, talk to someone at the counseling center about mental health services. In a crisis, these services can make the difference between dropping out and succeeding, so you want to know.

☑ How many minority students attend your university and do you have any special programs or services for them?

You can usually find out the number of minority students on the college website. But who are they? And what services does the school have for them? If you're a black teen from the inner city and you go to a historically black college where most of the students are from middle class and wealthier families, the fact that they're black may not be that helpful, for example. One of the most important facts you want to discover is the percentage of people like you (e.g., black males) who graduate in four years. If that number is high, the school is probably providing good support. If it's not, watch out.

☑ What kinds of extra-curricular activities do you have?

Colleges often offer a huge range of extra-curricular activities. You're bound to find something you like, unless you have a very specific interest, like fencing. If that's the case, make sure the school has it.

☑ Does social life revolve around the Greek system (fraternities and sororities)?

If it does, and you don't plan to join one, you might want to talk to some students about what the social life is like for non-Greeks.

☑ What does the area surrounding the university have to offer in terms of activities/social life/volunteer or work opportunities?

There are a lot of great colleges in the middle of nowhere. If you want to volunteer in a soup kitchen, intern at a major corporation, or go to concerts and museums, it will be tougher in places like that. Look into what kinds of events happen on campus, and if the college sponsors trips to nearby cities.

☑ How big a problem is crime on campus?

Most colleges are very safe. You can ask about crime, or go online to read the student newspaper or the local paper to get a general idea of the kinds of crimes that get reported.

☑ Do you have ROTC (Reserve Officers Training Corps)?

ROTC can help pay for your education, in return for serving in the armed forces after you graduate. If you plan to enroll in ROTC, make sure your college offers it.

Thanks to Mike Mallory, former director of admissions at the University of Virginia in Charlottesville, for sharing most commonly-asked questions.

Arnel Sencion

I Want To Go To a Historically Black College

By Regina Haywood

When choosing a college, ethnic diversity is important for many minority students. As an African-American high school senior, I've been interested in historically black colleges for years. That's why during the spring break of my junior year, I went on a week-long tour of black colleges in the Southeast. Along with 25 other high school students I visited eight colleges, including Spelman, Morehouse, Howard, and North Carolina A&T State.

I enjoyed the college tour immensely. I talked with students at the schools about their classes, how often they party, where they hang out and what goes on in the surrounding areas. I felt comfortable at each one, like I was at home with my brothers and sisters.

I was amazed at the excitement and pride I felt when I walked into a classroom and saw black young adults working hard learning subjects like psychology and calculus. I don't see this where I live. So many of my peoples are on the street corners, smoking weed and drinking.

After sitting in on their classes and eating in their cafeterias, I felt like a black college would be right for me. But which one?

I'm leaning more toward Howard University or North Carolina A&T State University. I want to be a broadcast journalist, so I took a tour of their TV and radio stations.

I was in love with both stations, which seemed to be well-organized and run professionally. Plus, the students were having a good time on the air, making shout-outs as DJs. It showed they liked their jobs and made me want to be part of the crew.

I also visited Hampton University and Norfolk State University with my family after the college tour. I want to apply

At some of the schools I've visited, I was like, "Where are the black people?"

to those universities as well because their radio stations also get top rankings among black colleges.

Despite how much I like the image of a black college, my school counselors and other adults are trying to sway me in the direction of state schools. They say that I can get scholarships as well as more financial aid there, and they think I should stay close to home so I won't have to spend a lot of money on airfare when it's time to see my family.

Keeping their advice in mind, I've visited predominantly white colleges, too, like Oswego in upstate New York, and Temple University in Philadelphia. I was impressed with the campuses, but at some of the schools I was like, "Where are the black people?"

At Oswego, for instance, only 9% of 7,900 students are minorities. That isn't enough of a black student population for me, particularly since blacks are included with other minorities in that figure.

I'm concerned that I may have a similar experience in college to what I've had in high school. My high school is predominantly Latino, and I feel alienated when I walk into the cafeteria and Latino students are speaking Spanish. As a non-Spanish speaker, I don't feel comfortable interrupting their conversations so that I can join the group.

Because of this, I've stopped myself from getting to know many of the students in my school. That's not to say that I don't have Latino friends, but it's not the same as hanging with my own people. Meanwhile, it's hard to feel united with the black students in my school when there aren't any black student organizations for us to join.

Keeping my high school experience in mind, I'm not that interested in being the minority again in college. The white schools I visited pale in comparison to what I've seen of the black college world.

Regardless of what my counselors say about getting aid from state colleges, black colleges have my heart. Even though many of them are under-funded, I will look into financial aid and also apply for outside scholarships. And, just to be on the safe side, I'm going to apply to some traditionally white institutions as well.

Regina was 18 when she wrote this story.

Jose Rodriguez

Seeing for Myself

By Latonya M. Pogue

When I was 8, I visited Smith College in Northampton, Massachusetts, to see my aunt graduate. When she went up to receive her degree, my mother said to me, "Look around. You might be up there some day." After the ceremony we walked around. The campus was clean and everybody seemed nice. I thought maybe I could graduate from Smith too—in about 14 years.

Three years later I visited another aunt who was starting her first semester at Howard University in Washington, D.C. One of the only things I remember is that her dorm was brand new and the rooms were extremely small. I couldn't believe this; I was 11 and I had a bigger room than my 18-year-old aunt.

I didn't ask anybody questions about those schools. I thought that I was too young and had plenty of time to think about college. I didn't even know what career I wanted to pursue. But I learned something about campus life just from looking around.

When I became a freshman in high school my teacher talked a lot about college and her alma mater, Columbia University in New York City. She said our class was taking a trip there, and I suddenly realized that I would be going to college myself in four years. My attitude changed. I definitely wanted to attend college like my aunts, but which one?

I wondered: How much does college cost? How hard is it to get in? Where should I go and where will I fit in? How is college life at a predominantly white school in the Northeast different from life at a historically black college or university in the South? I was determined to get some answers.

When my class arrived at Columbia we went into a cramped waiting area in one of the campus buildings. An older-looking, well-dressed African-American man talked to us about what Columbia looks at when deciding who'll be admitted. He said the university was academically demanding, that there would be lots of work and it would be hard. I get good grades in my high school classes and I'd heard this about college before. But hearing it directly from a college representative scared me.

Our hostess gave us her dorm key and told us to feel free to use her phone or play her CDs.

Then the man said that a good education costs a lot and Columbia was worth the money. How much, I wondered? And I listened intently until I heard him say that tuition alone cost about $37,000. After adding in room, board (meals), fees, and books, the cost for a year could be around $50,000!

That distracted me. I thought that there wasn't enough financial aid in the world to help me pay for all that. From then on everything the man said sounded muffled.

Afterward we had a question and answer session, ate lunch, took a tour of some of the campus, then left. We didn't get to see any of the classes and that disappointed me.

Later I decided to do some research to find out if Smith and Howard had tuition as high as Columbia's, and I found out that Smith does, but Howard costs much less. I started to realize the speaker was telling the truth about a good education being expensive, and decided I should not let that stop me. The education I get will be mine forever and not one person or thing will be able to take it away.

I still had more questions about college life. What would I be getting for all that money? And did I want to move to the South (most historically black colleges are there) or outside New York City at all? Did I want to be in the Northeast, Midwest, West—where?

But I didn't do any more research until last year when my school sponsored a trip for minority students to visit Cornell University (another Ivy League school like Columbia) in Ithaca, New York. When we arrived we were greeted by students who would be our hosts. Mine was a black student from Chicago who also was an RA (resident adviser) in her dorm.

The dorm was called Ujamaa and it was a clean, middle-sized, coed dorm where mostly black and Hispanic students lived. When we got there I noticed that some students left their doors wide open even when there was nobody there. Our hostess gave us her dorm key and told us to feel free to use her phone or play her music. As I went to bed that night I thought that this seemed like a very safe place.

In the morning my classmate and I started asking our hostess questions about classes. She told us that she loved all of her classes and got to know some of her professors. She invited us to go with her to one of her classes, but we had made plans to eat with some of our classmates so we went to the dining hall next to the dorm instead.

The dining hall had everything from a salad bar to a grill with fried foods to desserts. For breakfast there were hot and cold foods and fruit. When we sat down to eat, we thought that everyone would be laughing at us because we were still in high school and so young, but everybody was nice and polite. A group of students came over and started to tell us about the school and how much they enjoyed going there. Talking to some of the minority students about their experiences made me feel like I might fit in here.

Since we weren't going to classes, we decided to check out the campus after we ate. Downstairs from the dining hall, we found a game room and a grocery store. How convenient! We thought that students would have to travel all the way out to the city to have fun or buy groceries.

I'll get a better sense of whether or not I belong at a college if I visit and see for myself.

The next morning, breakfast was provided for us at the campus hotel. When we got inside the building, we got lost looking for the food and stumbled into a class for students studying hotel and restaurant management. Looking up from the floor of this big lecture hall, I saw rows and rows of people. It was unbelievable. My high school classes never have more than 30 students. Having large lecture classes didn't seem like such a good idea to me. Many students didn't seem to be listening. My friend and I ran out of the room and met up with the rest of our class. Then we left.

My visit made me want to apply to Cornell, but I still had questions about financial aid (my college book says Cornell costs as much as Columbia). Also: Is Cornell really as safe as it seemed and are other schools that safe? Is the food always as good as it was that weekend?

I still have other research to do. I wonder if other colleges organize visits for minority high school students like Cornell's. Do other schools let you spend the night in a dorm room? I am going to try to visit as many of the colleges that I am applying to as possible. Books can give me statistics and help me think of questions to ask, but I think I'll get a better sense of whether or not I belong at a college if I also visit and see for myself.

LaTonya was 16 when she wrote this story. She went on to graduate from Vassar College, in Poughkeepsie, New York.

Are You Ready for Dorm Life?

By Magda Czubak

As my senior year in high school gets closer, college often occupies my thoughts. So far, I don't know what I want to study or where, although I know I want to go to a good, big college with a lot of guys. My biggest concern is whether I should stay in my beloved New York City or go away to a school where I can live on campus.

On the one hand, if I leave New York City I would get away from my parents and finally have freedom. And I know I would enjoy experiencing life in a place with trees and lawns. On the other hand, if I go away to school, I would be leaving my friends and my job and the money it brings (as well as my boss and co-workers who are very special to me). Last but not least, I'd be sorry to leave my dog Saba. And, despite all the garbage and crime in New York City, I would miss it like hell.

To figure out if going away is worth these sacrifices, I interviewed several people who left New York to attend different colleges. They shared the ups and downs of living away from home, from the excitement of weeknight parties and new friends to the drudgery of washing their own clothes and eating bad hamburgers.

One of the high points of going away is living in a dorm and being independent. "There's nothing like living in a dorm," Jennifer Delaglio, 20, of Philadelphia College of Textiles and Science, told me enthusiastically. "I can go to parties on week nights. I have freedom from my parents."

One of Jennifer's best memories of dorm life was being "in pajamas in front of the guys and watching TV" the night before

One of the high points of going away is living in a dorm and being independent.

her finals. "A cool video came on and everyone started dancing. It's 2 o'clock in the morning. We have studying to do and we're dancing."

Ayisha Harvey, 18, a freshman at SUNY (State University of New York) New Paltz, also said she enjoys dorm life. "It's like having your own apartment," she said. "You come and go as you wish and your parents aren't there to say no."

But all that freedom comes with a price tag. Having your own place also means taking care of it and of yourself. "Nobody's looking over your shoulder to tell you to do little things," Ayisha told me.

For Ayisha, that meant shopping, doing the laundry, and cleaning her own room. "I had to do everything myself. Nobody was here to help me," she said. Although several people I interviewed complained about their new responsibilities, I think washing my clothes would be a small price to pay for all that freedom.

Unfortunately, as I learned from Jennifer, chores aren't the only down side of dorm life. Jennifer says the biggest problem can be the new roommate(s) with whom you'll have to share "rooms so small you can hardly move."

Jennifer's roommate problems began in her freshman year. "All of a sudden I had strangers using my stuff: stereo...make-up," she said. "One day I saw one of my roommates wearing my jacket and skirt. 'What the hell are you doing?' I asked. She said, 'You told me I could use your stuff. I thought it meant your clothes, too.' " After that, Jennifer decided the best way to deal with roommates was to "speak out or move out." After standing up for herself, Jennifer began to plan her move to another room.

If living with strangers doesn't work out, what about rooming with friends? In her sophomore year, Jennifer decided to try that approach. Things went better, but still weren't perfect. "I discovered it's hard to live with people whether you are friends or not," she said. "Everything was good except my new roommate got sloppy once in a while, and I have to have things neat."

Another problem was her roommate's boyfriend who Jennifer described as "a jerk." For example, "one night he had a couple of beers and he ended up throwing up in our room." This taught Jennifer an important lesson: "When choosing your roommate it's important to know if she has a boyfriend because the truth is you live with the boyfriend, too."

Just as important as dealing with roommates is making friends. Since my friends are very precious to me, one of my biggest concerns is whether I will make new ones I care about as much. Most of my interviews gave me hope that it's possible. Missy Omanoff, 23, a recent graduate of Syracuse University, said she met "friends for life" at college.

"The people you meet become your family," Missy told me. "We became friends quicker. It's because everyone has to start over, and because we see each other all the time." Missy was so happy with her new companions she didn't even feel like going home anymore. "Everything I needed and that was important to me was in Syracuse," she said.

Not everyone was that enthusiastic about their new relationships. Samantha Brown, 19, a freshman at Skidmore College, told me, "So far, I haven't met anyone who is as special to me as my old friends. I thought that it would be fun being away, but it's not. You are there completely alone." She hopes to transfer to New York University next fall.

Even if I can make new friends, I worry about keeping in touch with the old ones. But that wasn't hard for Jack Chmielowiec, 19, a freshman at SUNY Stony Brook. Jack said, "I didn't lose touch with them, we [just] spend less time together." Jack doesn't feel that anything has changed between him and

How far away the school is definitely affects how often you can come home to visit.

his high school friends. But maybe that's because his college is less than two hours away and he drives home for weekends.

Because Jennifer can't come home as often, she has to focus more on her new acquaintances. She admits, "I think I didn't maintain friends I had in high school. I hate to say it, but a lot separates us now. Some of my friends are already married and divorced or married and have babies." Jennifer was able to keep up two of her friendships by "phone calls and drop-in visits." Missy also remains in touch with some of her old friends, but added, "We do drift apart."

How far away the school is definitely affects how often most people can come home to visit. Because of the cost and time involved, Samantha can visit home only twice a month, although she'd like to go as often as Jack does. "I wish I could be there at least once a week," she said.

Of course not everyone wants to go home that often. Missy went home only for vacations and felt it was enough. Ayisha visits once every two months. "I don't even feel like going home more," she said. "You miss a lot of college life and you've got to pack."

Most of the people I spoke to agreed that one thing is definitely worse away from home: the food. Even though the cafeteria at her school is clean and pretty, Jennifer says "the food is really disgusting and unhealthy. The first year I lived on hamburgers. I gained 30 pounds!" Jack doesn't mind the food at Stony Brook, but he wishes he could have more choices. "They serve the same thing every day," he complained.

Of the five people I spoke to, only Samantha regretted going away to college. The rest recommend living on campus despite some discomforts. And I think coping with annoying room-mates sounds easier than dealing with my parents' curfews and demands.

But as much as I'd like to experience life in a quiet, clean place, I think leaving my friends, my brother, my co-workers, and my dog might be too painful. Therefore, the best solution for me would be to go to school here in New York City but to live on campus instead of at home.

Magda was 16 when she wrote this story. She went on to graduate from SUNY Binghamton, in upstate New York.

Skylar Kane Kraemer

How to Battle the Bureaucracy

By Cassandra Lim

It was mid-March of senior year and most of my classmates had started hearing from colleges. But even though we'd all filed our City University of New York (CUNY) applications online together in advisory class, I hadn't received a single letter.

I always thought the process of starting college would go smoothly because I had good grades in high school. But it turned out to be a nightmare, from finding out where I'd been accepted to registering for classes.

I checked my CUNY account online to see if there was a problem with my application and I found out my SAT score was missing from my application. That surprised me because my guidance counselor had said she would send in everybody's scores.

I sent in two copies of my score, but the computer still showed it as missing, so I had to ask my counselor to send it again. She told me to not worry so much and that I would start hearing from colleges before April. I trusted her for the last time.

By the end of the first week of April, my CUNY account said my application was complete. But I still hadn't heard from any of the colleges and I was scared that I wouldn't be accepted anywhere. So instead of waiting any longer, I took action.

After school one day, I went to Hunter College, my first choice, to find out my application status. Unfortunately, the gentleman in the office told me Hunter couldn't accept me because even though my GPA was high, my SAT scores were too low. As for the other four CUNY schools I'd applied to, he showed me my application status on his computer. The box next to each of the CUNY schools I'd applied to was blank.

I needed to prepare a list of questions so I wouldn't forget and be rushed out of the office.

"But I must have gotten into at least one CUNY," I thought anxiously. I decided to try another CUNY college and see if they knew my application status. I got back on the subway and headed to Queensborough Community College (QCC) since it was closest to my house.

I was nervous when I got to the campus because it was my first time there alone. I was afraid I might be discriminated against because I don't speak English well or because I look young. But I told myself I could do this without any help.

I asked for directions to the admissions center. There, a man told me I had been accepted, but because I'd put QCC as my fifth choice rather than my first choice, they hadn't sent me my acceptance letter yet.

Frustrated, I told the man to put QCC as my first choice. I didn't give myself time to think about whether a college I liked better might still send me an acceptance letter. I just wanted to avoid any further confusion.

I filled out some paperwork right then, and the man scheduled me for a placement test. When I got home that night, all my stress was gone. I didn't need to worry anymore about where I was going to college. But the confusion wasn't over yet.

Two weeks later, I scheduled an advisement appointment to talk about what classes I should take. I'm planning to major in nursing and transfer to a four-year college after I get my associate's degree.

When I arrived for my appointment, there were already four people waiting. Finally the lady at the front desk called my name. I followed the adviser into her cubicle, where she sat at her desk, messy with papers and files.

"I'm going to give you the same exact schedule as the student before you, since you and he have the same major," she said.

I looked at the schedule but there were only codes representing the classes, so I couldn't tell what they were. She didn't tell me anything about the classes, either. I noticed that one day a week, I didn't have a break between classes from 10 a.m. to 3 p.m. But when I told the adviser I wanted to change the schedule, she said, "It's hard to change it because a lot of classes are full. But you can go back home and change it online yourself."

She also told me that the computer showed I wasn't a New York resident, even though I've lived in Queens for four years, so I would have to go to the registrar center to prove myself. When I asked her what classes I needed to take for my major, she talked so fast that I didn't have a chance to open my mouth to ask anything else. Then she said, "You're all set."

I wanted to ask more questions, but I was so confused that I had nothing in my head. Afterwards I realized I needed to prepare a list of questions for my next appointment so I wouldn't forget and be rushed out of the office.

A week later I called the advisement department and said, "I would like to make an appointment to talk about my schedule with another adviser face to face." I gave the name of the first adviser I'd spoken to and said I wanted to speak to someone else this time.

"I have to talk to my director. I'll call you back," the lady on the other end said.

Another woman called me three hours later and asked me whether I really needed to speak to someone face to face.

"Yes," I replied firmly.

"Students can only make appointments right now for advisement or registering for classes. There's no time for you to come in to talk about your new schedule. But we can answer your questions by phone."

I remembered my list of questions and got it out of my book bag. I went through them one by one, asking how long the nursing program took and what the required classes were.

"I can't tell you everything right now, but you can go to our website and find everything you need in the catalog online," she said. She also said I could go to the registrar center to fix the long day on my schedule and to fix my residency mistake.

My advice to students is: when a problem occurs, don't ignore it. Ask for help.

By this point, I thought people in CUNY offices were mean and unhelpful. But when I went to the registrar center, I got lucky and met a nice lady who explained everything step by step. She showed me how to change my schedule online and answered all my questions so that I could do it myself at home. She even repeated her instructions to make sure I got it right. Then she directed me to another room where I was told I just needed to bring my green card or U.S. passport to resolve the residency issue.

I've had many experiences with college offices and I haven't even started classes yet. It's complicated and difficult, but the key is to be proactive. You can't depend on anyone to get things done for you—you have to do it yourself.

I've learned to look for people with smiling faces and to intro-duce myself before asking them questions, which I think makes them more likely to help. My advice to students is: when a prob-lem occurs, don't ignore it. Ask anyone for help, and if they can't help you, ask someone else until you get answers.

Cassandra was 18 when she wrote this story. She is now a student at Queensborough Community College in New York.

PART III:
Paying for It

Jessica Deng

Financial Aid 101

Finding the right school is one thing, but how do you pay for it? We talked to several experts who help teens in foster care find financial aid: John Emerson, senior manager of education for Casey Family Programs in Seattle, Dorothy Ansell assistant director of the National Resource Center for Youth Services in Tulsa, Oklahoma, and Eileen McCaffrey, executive director of the Orphan Foundation of America in Virginia. Their tips can work for anyone who's struggling to figure out how to finance a college education. Here's what they told us.

Q: What kinds of aid might I be eligible for?

A: All low-income students can apply for federal Pell Grants and state grants. There are also a wide variety of private scholarships, and you don't always have to meet an income requirement. Many private scholarships go unused because no one even bothers to apply. Even if your grades aren't excellent, you may still be eligible for scholarships, so check the requirements carefully. The college you choose to go to may also have its own scholarships and financial aid, so you should ask the financial aid officer what's available when you apply.

Q: How do I get started applying for financial aid?

A: To get the best financial aid package, it's important that you start the application process early, earn good grades, and be aggressive about digging up scholarships. It's also important to find a financial aid coach to help you get the money you'll need for school.

Juniors in high school who know where they want to go should call the college or vocational program they want to attend and make an appointment with a financial aid counselor. You should also speak to your high school guidance counselor. Tell guidance counselors and college financial aid counselors about your personal circumstances so they can target scholarships, grants and other financial aid especially designed for you. Then, during the fall of your senior year, start filling out the FAFSA.

Q: I always hear people talking about that. What exactly is the FAFSA?

A: The FAFSA (Free Application for Federal Student Aid) determines whether you can get Pell Grants, Federal Supplemental Educational Opportunity Grants, Federal Work Study and low-interest loans. That means it's a must. You can find it online at www.fafsa.ed.gov.

It's important to have your financial aid coach look over your FAFSA application before you submit it, just to make sure you haven't made any mistakes.

Q: Can I receive financial aid if I'm not a full-time student?

A: Yes, usually you can get some financial aid if you carry at least nine credits. (In most colleges, each class counts for three credits.) If you qualify, you can also get a Pell Grant from the federal government for part-time enrollment. This is a good option if you want to get an education but don't feel you can handle a full-time course load.

Q: I'm afraid to take out a loan. What can I do?

A: It's actually a good idea to borrow to invest in your future, as long as you borrow only what you need. It's OK to arrange a low-interest educational loan through your college financial aid counselor and graduate owing $5,000. Just make sure you really do get your degree or certificate!

Borrowing money to get a degree from an inexpensive public college is a good investment. Think more carefully about borrowing tens of thousands of dollars to attend a private college. And beware of expensive private trade schools: borrowing money to attend these kinds of schools can put you deep in debt before you know it. As a general rule, never borrow money to attend a private trade school.

> *It's actually a good idea to borrow money and invest in your future, as long as you borrow only what you need.*

Q: If I want to become a hairdresser, mechanic or dental assistant, am I still eligible for financial aid?

A: In most cases, yes—but again, you should be careful when you choose a vocational/technical trade school. Many of these programs are extremely misleading, so be very skeptical. Before you enroll in a school that gives you a credential to be a nurse, dental assistant, mechanic, radio D.J. or any other certificate, interview people who do hiring for the kind of job you hope to have. Ask them if the school you're interested in provides good training. If they say "no," ask which schools do and go to one of them instead.

You want to be confident that you can land a good job when you complete your training. Instead of a private trade school, consider a local community college or non-profit program that offers similar training. If you realize the school isn't any good and leave, you will lose time and waste money.

How to File Your FAFSA

The fastest way to fill out the FAFSA is on the Web. If you don't have Internet access, ask your guidance counselor for an application. When you fill it out online, start out by getting a PIN (Personal Identification Number) at the FAFSA website: www.fafsa.ed.gov.

Check your email constantly after you apply for your PIN, since they'll send it within a couple of days. After you get your PIN, you can fill out the online form.

You have to wait until January 1 to file your financial aid application for the next academic year, but do it as soon as possible after that. (Don't wait to find out if you were accepted into any schools.)

When filling out the FAFSA, you'll need your Social Security number, driver's license, your parents' W-2 form and federal income tax return (or yours if you're independent), untaxed income records, current bank statements, and current business and mortgage information. And if you aren't a U.S. citizen, you'll need your green card.

After you email your FAFSA, you'll receive information about your state's program for financial aid. To qualify for state financial aid, you usually have to be enrolled at an approved in-state college. If you go to an out-of-state school, you won't get the state money.

Jessica Deng

There's Always a Choice

By Xavier Reyes, as told to *Represent*

In high school I lived in a group home, and a lot of staff and counselors there had high hopes for me. I was in special education but I fought to get out so that I could graduate at 16.

I attended an alternative high school that had smaller classes. I really liked that. The teachers focused on me and really wanted to see me excel. I paid attention in class, and I knew how to use words well. My college counselor told me I needed to apply for scholarships. That was a big thing: having people at my back who encouraged me.

Back then, the things that worried me about college were my lack of money, doubts about whether I could handle it academically, and my own stigma about being in foster care. Plus, I worried about making it on my own. I didn't want to leave one system just to end up in another (like welfare).

I graduated salutatorian and I was accepted to Pace University in New York. I enrolled at Pace, but I wasn't ready for it. I soon dropped out. I'd received a renewable $1,000 scholarship from the United Federation of Teachers to attend Pace. After I dropped out, I lost that. I continued working, but I felt pressure from everyone—friends, family, mentors—to go back to college. So five years after I graduated from high school, I enrolled at a different college.

I was not making enough money, and every semester was a challenge. I resisted taking out loans. After a year I transferred to a community college. I hated it—it felt like high school. But I stuck it out for two semesters before I dropped out and went to work full-time.

Don't wait for someone to show you the way when it comes to college. Put some time into figuring things out.

At that point, I was definitely more concerned about my own livelihood than an education, because by then I was aging out of the system, and the comfort I had known with foster care was gone. So it was sort of pick and choose—do you want to be educated or do you want to survive? I wanted to survive. I needed to work and I needed a place to live. I needed to get myself together. School had to wait.

Eventually my home environment became more stable. I was living on my own and the bills were coming in, but I was in a much better mental state to handle school and the responsibilities that came with it. I applied to Baruch College and got a $20,000 scholarship. Baruch accepted about half the credits I'd earned already.

My scholarship paid for my tuition, but I had to pay for my own books and living expenses. Money was tight, and, because I was living independently, my choice was get a loan or drop out again. I didn't want to take out loans, but in the end I had to. Looking back, loans aren't really a bad thing. I've learned that an educational loan is really an investment in my own future.

I did my full four years at Baruch and finally graduated with a degree in Public Affairs. The whole time I worked full time and had a full class load.

Foster care always gave me the message that I didn't have choices. The fact is there is always a choice. Today I sit on the committee that awarded me my scholarship to attend Baruch. I see a lot of applications that don't show much effort. You can tell that an adult just told the kid to fill out the application, but the kid didn't really try.

A lot of times, no one sits down with the students and helps them with their essay, makes sure that it looks "college ready." No one's guiding them. Their responses on the applications are very generic.

I've learned that you have to distinguish yourself, especially if you want to get into a particular field or college and get scholarships. A little effort goes a long way. My advice would be to not wait for someone to show you the way when it comes to college. Ask and keep asking and put some time into figuring things out. It's not easy, but in the end it really is you who has to make the choice.

Xavier graduated from college and earned a master's degree in business. He now works for a major media company.

Jane Heaphy

Take Charge of Your College Bills

By Marci Bayer

Receiving your financial aid package is only the beginning. Many college students have to figure out what their financial aid will cover and not cover, choose loans, and limit spending. Fortunately, programs like the OPTIONS Center in New York City helps students figure out the college application process—including financial aid—free of charge. I interviewed director Jane Heaphy, who has more than 17 years of experience counseling students, to get her advice on managing finances in college.

Q: What should students do when they get to college to make sure they're on top of their financial aid?

A: Meet with your financial aid counselor in person, just to say,

"Can we go over my plan so I'm really clear on it?" You want to feel educated on the aid you're receiving, because you're going to have to renew your financial aid every single year. Also, if the financial aid staff knows you and they can go the extra mile for you, that's a good investment of your time.

Q: What's the most common source of confusion when it comes to financial aid?

A: An important thing to know is that "financial aid" includes grants (which are scholarships and not paid back), loans, and work-study. When a school tells you, "We'll cover you with full financial aid," you still want to know: what kind of aid is it, how much are you borrowing, how much are you expected to earn in a job once you're there.

Q: Can you offer any advice for dealing with the bureaucracy of financial aid offices?

A: Keep a paper trail—a copy of your FAFSA and letters from the college, so you have a fat folder of all your financial aid information. If there's some problem, you want to be able to defend your situation by having all your documents.

Q: What can students do if financial aid doesn't meet all their expenses?

A: Advocate for yourself. Send a letter saying, "I'd like you to consider me for additional financial aid," and explain more about your life situation. Sometimes it works and sometimes it doesn't, but it's an effort of 15 minutes writing the letter, and if you get $2,000 more, it was worth it.

Q: Would you advise students to take out loans?

A: It depends. If my choice was to take out some loans or not go to college, I would advise everybody to take out some loans. However, I want students to feel really informed about what their responsibilities are. If after you leave college you're spending, say, $1,200 a month paying back your loans, then it may have been financially counterproductive. There are some loan calculators on www.finaid.org that will help you break the total amount you're considering into the monthly amounts you'll pay for 10 years after you graduate—I find those helpful.

Q: How should a student evaluate different types of loans?

A: Loans from the federal loan program have the lowest interest rates and make the most sense. Then there are private loans, from different financial institutions. In my experience, if you're getting into the private loan area, you probably want to reconsider. With the federal loan program, you can get up to about $24,000 per year. If you're borrowing more than that, I would be very cautious.

Meet with your financial aid counselor in person, just to say, "Can we go over my plan so I'm really clear on it?"

Q: What should students do to manage their money in college?

A: When you get to college, credit cards are almost thrown at you, when you actually don't have the ability to pay up yet. It can become an all-consuming kind of debt. So be educated about credit cards, and learn money-saving tips from students who've been there a couple of years already. Buy books online or from other students. If you've already paid for your meal plan, eat in the cafeteria. Additionally, you have to pay for the occasional tube of toothpaste or the bus ticket home, so make sure that you open a bank account when you get to campus.

Q: What do you advise for those who must work to pay for school?

A: Certainly the extra cash can keep the pressure off. I also think it can get you more connected on campus if you get a work-study job—those can be good networking opportunities. It becomes a problem when you're working so much that you can't be the student you want to be. Plan it out so that your hours are as part-time as possible.

Q: What's most important to remember when dealing with finances during college?

A: Before you sign a loan or fill out forms, don't be afraid to ask questions. So much of the time, we think we're supposed to know things, but actually it's new to us. New college students are all learning about financial aid, so it's critical to ask questions.

Marci graduated from high school and now attends the University of Maryland.

Kat Morris

Take Our Advice: Financial Tips

"If you need to go to the college financial aid office, get there early—as if you were buying concert tickets. If you have a class that starts at 10 a.m. and you get on that line at 9, chances are you're not going to make it to class that day."

—**Hector**, 22, *sophomore*

"Have a good relationship with the financial aid office staff. Say hi to them every once in a while. Tell them, "Your hair looks nice today." When they have to do the paperwork, they might be more likely to go the extra mile for you."

—**Pauline**, 21, *junior*

College is a business—remember that, first and foremost. If you fail, you are paying to fail, because they want their money either way. If you don't know what you're doing in class, get tutoring. If a financial aid counselor isn't helping you, go to someone else. Don't wait until it's too late.

—Tasha, 20, sophomore

"I have a checking account with online access, so it's easy for me to see how much money I have and think about how much of it I should spend. I also write down all my expenses in a balance booklet so I can see how I'm spending my money. I think college students should have a bank account, because cash can be easily stolen and it's more tempting to spend it. But be careful about going to other banks' ATMs because banks often charge big fees when you don't use your own bank's ATM."

—Teyu, 18, freshman

"Too many people, me included, spend money on things they want but don't really need. It's always a good idea to save extra money for books or other things you need unexpectedly."

—Otis, 19, freshman

"Budget your money carefully. Before buying something, ask yourself, 'Do I really need it?' and, 'How will this benefit me?'"

—Te-Li, 20, junior

PART IV:
Surviving College

Skylar Kane Kraemer

In My Own Hands

By Orlando Hawkins

For me, high school was a struggle, a constant psychological battle. I was haunted by past experiences in the foster care system—abuse, my difficulty maintaining positive relationships, and most importantly, not being able to be myself. I felt held back many times, which caused me to think negatively about myself.

No one ever told me how vital school is. I would sometimes observe my classmates, and wonder why some people worked so hard in high school. I just couldn't see the purpose. I'd see people trying hard and getting nervous in speeches for student government elections. I thought it was lame. Some would go out of their way to participate in clubs, organize events, and do volunteer work. I didn't realize how important these activities—and the things you learn while doing them—were to your college applications. No one explained to me that colleges looked for well-rounded people.

I realized that I would never understand the world of an ordinary high school student. My world was full of hatred and terror while everyone else's seemed to be full of joy and pleasure. I resented them because they had everything that I wanted, such as living a decent life and being intellectual.

I knew I wanted to go to college, but I didn't know exactly why I wanted to go, or what I wanted to do as a career. I think that was because I didn't have someone I could turn to when I needed help. I ended up attending a large community college in California. I came to college with the same apathy that I had in high school.

My lack of preparation almost led me to a disastrous first semester. I thought I was fooling myself in trying to become successful. But my biggest fear was ending up like the rest of my family. There weren't a lot of models for success in my family, and I decided that I had to do great in college if I didn't want to end up like them.

The hardest part of starting college was realizing that I had to do everything myself. From picking classes to making appointments to see an academic adviser, I came to realize that no one was going to hold my hand. During the fall semester, the only college office I visited (I knew it by heart) was the financial aid building, because I didn't know how I was going to pay for my classes and books.

Since I was not used to studying, I often found myself on MySpace or hanging out with people I knew from high school instead of doing my work. These old high school habits were hard to break. But in my fifth week of college, that mindset changed.

I was sitting in my sociology class, and my professor was lecturing us about student success in community college. Suddenly, he said something that caught my attention. In his 15 years at the college, he said, he'd only seen one African-American male graduate and transfer to a four-year university. I was the only

African-American in the class, and he looked right at me as he spoke.

Strangely, I didn't feel angry, because I realized that the professor was telling the truth. I just felt embarrassed about being put, yet again, in a category of people who have a stigma attached to them. Because I was in foster care, some people thought it was more likely that I'd end up homeless than in college. Yet here I was, sitting in this classroom. Still, I couldn't deny the fact that the African-American graduation rate at my school was dismally low. I felt like I had something to prove. I felt challenged.

As the professor continued, I suddenly had a newfound energy, a feeling of enlightenment that was telling me to just keep moving forward and prove the stereotype wrong. I'd never felt this before. After the class, I went up to the professor and told him, "Thanks, now I know what I need to do."

"You're welcome," he replied. I had the sense, though, that he didn't understand why I was thanking him.

I left the classroom and headed to the library. The only thing that was going through my mind was the professor's words: He'd seen only one African-American male graduate in 15 years. In my head, those words were ringing a bell,

Looking right at me, my professor said he'd only seen one African-American male graduate and transfer to a four-year university.

a bell like the one that lets you know, "Hey it's time to go to class," but this time it was saying, "Hey, Mr. Hawkins, it's time for great things to happen for you, so get a move on."

As I entered the library, I spotted an open computer and automatically started walking toward it. Then I hesitated. Would I get on and check MySpace, or would I actually be true to myself and start picking up the slack by starting to take my studies seriously? I decided to give in to old habits and jump on the computer.

What happened next is something I'll never forget. I tried

multiple times to log on and I couldn't get through. I stood there, perplexed but also suddenly observant in a way I hadn't been before. I looked around at everyone else who was on the computer for reasons other than college work and I had a revelation. I realized that if I did not stay true to myself by sticking to my goals, I would end up like the rest of these people and remain unsuccessful. So I walked away.

I walked further and further into the library and each step I took felt like an accomplishment. I was making the decision not to be influenced by pop culture media because it would only distract me. I found an empty table, took my sociology book out, and started reading about different cultures.

I caught on to the material pretty quick and felt good about myself because I was learning something new, and I was actually interested in it. As I sat there, I had the distinct feeling that, in time, something great was going to happen to me.

A few weeks after my revelation, my sociology professor got into an accident. He feel off a ladder and broke some ribs, both his wrists, and his nose. Although I felt sorry for him, his absence allowed me to study more and catch up. I'd been bombarded with homework because he went at a very fast pace. I'd been worried about having to drop the class, but his absences allowed me to catch up my studies and do better on the exam. That was a confidence booster, and I learned so much more than I would have.

Our class eventually got a substitute professor to replace our old one. This professor was much easier to understand and very fun. She was the perfect professor to correlate with my newfound motivation. I could actually keep up with her lessons and she provided excellent examples. She taught so well that I thought about majoring in sociology.

She made me look at society from a different perspective, and I've come to realize that everyone is different, myself included. I remember reading a novel by Virginia Woolf called *To The*

Lighthouse. In this book, Woolf allows the readers to enter the mind of her characters, revealing who they are, and, most importantly, their differences. The novel spoke to me and reflected how I viewed life. Everyone puts on a mask, but who someone is, not who he portrays himself to be, is the most important aspect of a person. I realized differences are normal and OK because you can learn from them.

> *I began to observe other students and realized that they knew more about things than I did because they took their studies outside of the classroom.*

Seeing the world from a philosophical perspective made me look at things differently. I realized that it is better to be a critical thinker than someone who is just book smart. I began to observe other students and realized that they knew more about things than I did, not only because they studied the material but because they took their studies outside of the classroom. I decided to develop that same habit.

I decided I had to get over my shyness and start surrounding myself with positive, intellectual people. I realized that my life was in the balance. I had to learn to live in the present, no matter what had happened in my past. Once I started thinking that way, things got easier.

I got back into reading for myself and realized that I was able to keep up in conversation with adults outside of school at places like jazz festivals and restaurants. Most importantly, I was able to connect with my professors. I could now have discussions with my professors about academic stuff and I felt more like a grown-up.

I discovered that I was learning more about the world and a lot of things started to make sense to me that hadn't before. For the first time in my life, people were actually calling me the smart person.

As I began to study more and more, my grades began to improve, not just because I studied out of the book but because I was interacting with other people on campus. My spring semester, I was no longer timid and I felt like I was going to become a great individual. My confidence was at its peak. For the first time in my life I could actually say I was happy. My world was in the palm of my hand and I was rotating it.

Besides my improved confidence and connections to other students, what really helped things go more smoothly was knowing where my resources were. It started when I met a kind-hearted scholarship coordinator the first week of spring semester. She told me about scholarships especially for students in foster care and encouraged me to get more involved on campus. She said students who are more involved have higher success rates than students who are not.

I learned that college is not only about grades; the main thing is to obtain knowledge.

It just so happened that my campus was having Club Week, so I joined multiple clubs. I ended up co-founding our campus philosophy club and another called "Don't Tread On Me," which raises awareness about human trafficking.

I also attended a couple of school events and met with important people like the college vice-president and academic counselor. Now I know at least one person from the financial aid office, the career and transfer centers, the vice president's office, the two deans of counseling, the Educational Opportunity Program—the list goes on. I discovered that the resources are there; all you have to do is go out there and use them to your advantage.

Most importantly, I learned that college is not only about grades; the main thing is to obtain knowledge. Too often, the emphasis today is on making money—not on the learning experience. But the chance to gain knowledge is what turned things around for me, not the promise of a career that would make me rich. I now find it fun to learn new things. For example, I realized that I was interested in debate after taking a political science class when the presidential campaign was going on.

I ended my spring semester with a 3.9 GPA, and I made the President's List. I now have my sights set on obtaining my bachelor's degree and eventually attending a top law school. I might become an attorney for foster youth or perhaps a defense attorney. Eventually I want to go into politics and become a senator or a legislator to reform the system for the benefit of the people. None of this would have been possible if I hadn't started making connections with people and approaching college with an open mind.

Orlando is still in college, working toward
his bachelor's degree.

Stephanie Wilson

Take Our Advice: Adjusting to College

"My first couple of days, I was like, 'Do I belong here?' Because, I kid you not, there were kids talking about this book they'd read or that philosopher they liked. But while they were very intellectual, they were also very 'yeah, let's go out and party.' I like to go out but I don't drink. So it was kind of like, 'Where do I fit in here?'

"For me, just seeing my grades made me feel like I belonged. I came to realize that maybe they were feeling insecure like I was and maybe that was why they decided, well, let me bring up everything that I ever learned—ever—to impress people."

—*Desiree*, 19, *sophomore*

"I'm from New York and I went all the way down to New Orleans to volunteer, and on a whim I decided to stay for college. I don't think I took into account the distance. I had no family around and there were times when I was just so lonely, so confused.

"To deal with it, first I cried, and then I remembered why I'd come—to get an education, to learn about myself and the world. And if you stay focused on why you came to college, then you should be OK."

—*Tasha*, 20, sophomore

"During my first month of college, I felt that none of my professors were going to like my work because I had no clue what I was doing. I worried so much about getting negative feedback from my professors that it would keep me from finishing my assignments. I had to learn to speak up and ask questions when I was unsure of something instead of waiting until it was too late."

—*Pedro*, 21, sophomore

"The hardest thing for me about adjusting to college has been the writing. In high school, it was easy for me to get A's and B's on essays, but in college I've been getting C+'s. I didn't understand why. Now I go to tutoring and ask friends to read over my essays, and my writing is improving."

—*Teyu*, 18, freshman

"Social life in high school was all about fitting in with the crowd, gossiping and fighting. Boring! In college things have a more moderate tone and nobody broadcasts other people's business enough to make it a big deal. Thank God for that, eh?"

—*Otis*, 19, freshman

"In high school they cut you a lot of slack, but in college if you don't turn in your homework on time, prepare to fail."

—*Pauline*, 21, junior

"In high school, whether I spoke up in class or not really didn't make a difference. But in college I've made a 180-degree transformation. I've started raising my hand, I get into class debates, and sometimes even challenge the teacher when I think it's necessary. Participation counts in college."

—*Teyu*, *18, freshman*

Percyell Smith

Freshman Year: A Fresh Start

By Ferentz Lafargue

I can't front. When my first semester of college started, I was lost. I had just finished a subpar (at least I thought so) four years of high school. As a matter of fact I was still checking my mailbox for the letter telling me that my graduation was an accident. I kept expecting that I was going to have to return my diploma and report back to Jamaica HS in Queens, NY.

Luckily, that never happened and I soon found out that college is very different from high school. Well, at least it can be if you want it to. First of all you get a fresh start. You don't have to walk into class and act like a clown or a hardhead.

In high school, you have to do that because a lot of your friends from junior high are there and you want to impress them. But in college nobody there knows you. They don't know that you're a clown, and if you are they don't care, because they're there to learn. You get to be yourself, because that's really all that's asked of you.

Well, you also have to do the work. The teachers—excuse me, professors—don't play around. If they do, you're in trouble, because remember, you're the one who's paying for the classes.

There are two types of college classes. First, there's the type like my English class that are practically discussion groups. You're given a book to read and all that is asked of you is to be able to analyze and discuss it. (That means, of course, you have to actually read the book and think.)

Then there are the dreaded lecture courses, where you sit for two hours while the professor talks to her heart's content on any subject, while you take notes. These classes are usually held in rooms the size of an auditorium, and there are at least 200 people in them, so it's a mission just to get to a seat. Well, if you are an urban public high school student, you should be right at home in these types of classes.

One of the best things about college, for me at least, is that doing the work is fun (most of the time). I've learned that if I do my best, something good will always come out of it. For example, one day during my English class something came over me and I just started blurting out literary terms—foils, juxtapositions, ironies. If it was in the story I found it. It was clear to everyone that I'd understood what I'd read.

A professor who'd been observing the class came by and told me how bright I was. After she finished praising me, my professor asked me if I'd be interested in a fellowship (like a scholarship) for English majors. It was after this conversation that I realized that I have a gift and it should be worked on.

I began taking my work more seriously, because success seemed closer. It wasn't like in high school where I lacked the confidence to pursue awards, and when I did it was usually half-heartedly so that if I didn't get them I could always say, "Well, of course not, I didn't try."

And college isn't all work. Another important part is being able to make new friends, and if you can make them on your own terms it's even better. (Meaning that you're getting along with everyone and having fun while still keeping up with your work.)

In high school I was mad quiet (when I wasn't clowning around, that is) and it made people think that I was conceited. Kids were always uncomfortable around me, because they thought I didn't like them, and, to be honest, I didn't go out of

One of the best things about college is that doing the work is fun (most of the time).

my way to make any friends either. When I got into college I was determined to change this, so I followed a simple rule: "Open up and whoever wants to come in, will come in." And it works.

I'm having the time of my life in college. I'm even glad that I decided to stay at home instead of going away to school. When people come and tell me how much fun I could be having if I had gone away or gone to a bigger school, I don't care. Those people never mention how expensive dorms get to be, or the possibility of having the roommate from hell or how pizza and take-out Chinese food tend to lose their appeal after a while.

There is one thing that I've missed out on since starting college and that's sleep. In fact, the key to success in college is to sleep whenever and wherever you get a chance, because you won't get the chance too often. In fact, now that I've finished this article, it's time for my nap.

Ferentz was 19 when he wrote this story. He graduated from college, got a PhD from Yale University, and became a college professor.

YC Art Dept.

Dr. Mark Noonan, Dr. Marta Effinger-Crichlow, Dr. Janet Liou-Mark,
Dr. Robin Isserles and Dr. Reginald Blake

Meet Your Professors

There are a lot of things that can be intimidating when you start college, but your professors shouldn't be one of them. We spoke to five professors who are doing their best to help their students succeed in college: Dr. Reginald Blake, assistant professor of physics at New York City College of Technology (City Tech); Dr. Marta Effinger-Crichlow, assistant professor of African-American studies at City Tech; Dr. Robin Isserles, assistant professor of sociology at Borough of Manhattan Community College; Dr. Janet Liou-Mark, associate professor of mathematics at City Tech and Dr. Mark Noonan, assistant professor of English at City Tech.

Q: What do you consider your responsibility as a professor to be?

Dr. Reginald Blake: To teach in an exciting way and to really help students become learners. I'm very concerned about my students and I often become a mentor to them. It's not just what happens in the classroom. Oftentimes I find myself dealing with other issues they face that hinder the way they perform in class.

Dr. Marta Effinger-Crichlow: To provide a safe environment in the classroom, where students feel comfortable sharing their ideas with other people. I want students to admit, "I don't understand."

Dr. Janet Liou-Mark: With math, I deal with a lot of students who come with bad feelings from past experiences, with a sense that they're going to fail. I like to make them believe that even if you failed math in high school, you can still learn.

Effinger-Crichlow: Years ago someone told me this proverb: Bring more to the table than your appetite. I tell my students up front, "This is a give and take experience. What do you have to bring to the table at the end of the day?" Questions, remarks—you've got to bring something.

Also, if you're with me for three months, you've got to know something about me. So sometimes I'll refer to a story my grandfather told me years ago. I think it breaks down a barrier. I don't want my students to be frightened by me. I want them to be open and feel safe.

Q: What problems do you see students struggling with the most?

Dr. Robin Isserles: Time management is a huge problem. To get financial aid, you need to take 12 credits, which is hard to handle with also working full-time and perhaps also full-time family responsibilities. I recommend to my students to take as few classes as possible, especially at the beginning.

Dr. Mark Noonan: Many students never spent the time to work on the fundamentals. I'm always struck by profound thinkers who can't get their thoughts down on paper adequately because they're held back by little grammar and style issues, which simply take practice.

Q: What do students need to do to pass your classes?

Isserles: They have to be not just physically present, but attentively participating and coming in prepared. A lot of preparation happens outside the class. Many new students don't really get that. When they calculate how many classes to take, they think they can fit this class in with their work schedule and picking up the kids—but they forget about all the hours necessary for weekly readings, exam preparation and writing papers.

Effinger-Crichlow: At times, students don't do well when it comes to the first paper. But I always give everyone an opportunity to revise. If I see that you're making an effort, I take that into consideration. Some students will do a revision three or four times—to see a paper go from a D to a B after a month or so, that's exciting.

Liou-Mark: They need to do their homework. For math, no matter if you understand it during lecture, you need the extra practice.

Q: Do you expect students to approach you outside of class? Does knowing a student personally affect how you evaluate them?

Effinger-Crichlow: Oh, definitely. Maybe they didn't get to ask a question during class or they need me to clarify something. Coming to see me says that you are engaging, you are participating in the process, and that's beyond the one hour and 15 minutes of class.

Noonan: By contract, full-time professors have established office hours. I think there are two factors that prevent students from coming. One is the intimidation factor. The other one is that a lot of students think it's uncool to be seen being friendly with a professor. Especially young men—culturally, they've been coded to be a little more independent. But the sooner you get over those two factors, the better it's going to be for everyone.

Isserles: I tell my students that I can't make this promise, but if you're on the cusp of a B+ and an A- and you come to office hours, there's a good chance you might get that A-. You separate yourself from the other 40-some-odd students I have in my class.

Q: What should students do if they fail a paper or an exam?

Isserles: Sit down with the professor. After my first exam, I make a mandatory meeting with all my students who failed. I tell them, "I'm not going to berate you. I want to find out what went wrong."

For those students who studied and failed, we go through: How long did you study? Where did you study? Were you keeping up with the readings? That way I'm sort of talking through what should be done, and they don't have to tell me, but they can figure out, "Oh I didn't do that; I did do that but I didn't do enough of that."

We're going to be thrilled that you failed an exam and came in to see us. Because then we're going to think this student is really serious, and we can work together for you to come out with a decent grade at the end of the semester.

Q: What are some "do's and don't's" for incoming college students?

Effinger-Crichlow: Some "don't's" are consistently coming to class late, having your cell phone go off, going outside class to answer your cell phone—I will follow you. Another don't is plagiarizing. Going to Google, cutting and pasting something, as if I don't have a computer.

Also, at the end of the semester I usually ask my students to do final presentations. There was one young woman who didn't feel comfortable speaking in front of others. We worked really long hours on her presentation. She stood before the class and there were two individuals making fun of her during her presentation. I don't know if you ever saw the movie The Exorcist? I went off. I stopped her presentation and demanded that the two students who were making fun of her leave my class. When you disrespect my students in class, I really get angry.

Blake: Find out if there are any opportunities for doing research with a professor. It opens up a whole world of academia and learning to you. Intern in someone's office, even if you're making copies. You could end up with your name on a paper that's being published.

Isserles: Ask for help. When you miss a class, get the notes. Ask someone what went on in class. Communicate with the professor. Send an email—my daughter's sick and I don't have backup daycare. Show an interest in what you missed.

And learn from each other. In my undergraduate studies I had a small seminar and on one of the first days of class, the professor asked us all to observe what was happening. Every time he spoke we were writing notes. And as soon as somebody asked a question, the pens went down. We couldn't gain any insight, any knowledge from each other. That made such a mark on me. I tell my students every semester: keep your pens up, keep your ears open when your classmates speak. I don't know everything. And your fellow students sitting here know a lot.

Kingslee Gourrick

My First Semester: Overworked, Underpaid, and Unprepared

By Troy Shawn Welcome

When I was younger, I used to imagine what my life after high school would be like. I saw myself going away to a small, supportive college, living in a dormitory, meeting new people, and having new experiences. I never thought that I would have any difficulty merging onto the highway of adult life. Now almost a year has passed since I graduated from high school and I've found that making it in the world of responsibilities, bills, priorities, and decisions is harder than I thought.

When the time came to apply to college, I was sure of only one thing—I wanted to go away to school. I never wanted to attend school in New York City where I grew up because there are too many distractions here. I worried that I would be hanging out with my friends too much and not devoting enough time to studying. So I decided to apply to a few SUNY (State University of New York) schools and to Sarah Lawrence College, a private school about 30 minutes from the city in Bronxville, New York. As a last resort, I also applied to some CUNY (City University of New York) schools.

I found out about Sarah Lawrence from the guidance counselor at my high school. He went to college there and told me that the school was famous for its writing program. Since I was what some people considered a born writer, he thought Sarah Lawrence would be perfect for me.

After I visited Sarah Lawrence's campus for a weekend I agreed with him. Most of the people were friendly and found time in their schedules to entertain me. I went to a party on campus, played pool with some other students, and saw a movie in the campus theater. I liked the atmosphere.

While I was there, I also attended a couple of classes so I could get an idea of what the work was like. I went to a literature class on Saturday morning and most of the people there looked as if they had slept in the classroom, including the professor. It shows a lot when people are comfortable enough to go to class in what looks like their pajamas. I've always felt that small, comfortable classes served me better than large, impersonal ones. I left that Sunday with a love for Sarah Lawrence and the idea that I could spend the next four years there.

Unfortunately, I wasn't accepted, and that's when my problems started. I wasn't particularly interested in going to any of the public SUNY colleges—I hadn't even completed the applications. I had thought I was a shoo-in for Sarah Lawrence. I had only considered SUNY in the first place because my counselor had told me that it's better to apply to a lot of schools so that I'd have some choices. I guess he was right.

Since I had completed my CUNY applications, I still had the

option of going to a city school. I had heard many good things about Baruch from my counselor, so it became my first choice. Luckily, Baruch also chose me.

At first, I was excited to know that I'd be going to Baruch. Actually, I was excited to be going anywhere. It was extremely important to me to get a college education because I'd be only the second person in my family to attend college. (My brother was the first.) In all the excitement, I can't say that I really envisioned what the first day would be like, but I sure didn't expect what I saw at registration.

When I walked into the registration building at Baruch, I experienced what I considered "college hell." There were people on lines, on stairs, in front and in back of me. They all looked confused and upset. I wondered what the problem was.

Most students, myself included, just went in, went to class and then went to work. That wasn't what I wanted.

I had a 3 o'clock appointment, so I strolled over to the right line, secure in the knowledge that I already had my schedule planned out. I had attended a summer orientation where I was given the fall semester course catalogue and instructed on how to arrange my schedule.

I soon found out that none of that mattered. The guy circling the room wasn't handing out college leaflets; he was handing out lists of available courses. Every 15 minutes, he came around with a new list—it seemed that the longer I stood on line, the more courses got closed. Wait a minute! All the classes I was planning to take had been filled. What was I supposed to do now?

My mind was scrambling for answers when I began to notice the two other packed lines that were ahead of the one I was on. Those people had appointments for 1:45 and 2:30. The majority of them were squatting on the floor—they had been waiting so long that their legs wore out. It was then that I got the courage to glance at my watch. It was already 4:30 and I was frustrated (my appointment was for 3:00 p.m., remember?). And I had to be at work by 6.

I changed my schedule two more times while on line and then three more as I sat with the counselor. Then I walked toward the cashier to pay for the scraps I ended up with. I was given African studies, psychology, and the usual math and English courses.

By the time I was three weeks into the semester, I was already having to force myself to go to class. My African studies course was one of the straws that broke the camel's back. It was a lecture class, which should've been easy. We just had to read certain chapters in our textbook along with attending lectures.

Since I hardly had time to work full-time and read books, I tried to get as much as I could from the lectures. But the professor had a very thick accent and I needed an interpreter to understand 90% of what was being said. That's when I started falling behind.

My psychology class was better. Even though there were about 500 students, the two professors who taught it always added a dash of humor to their lectures, which made it fun. But the fact that it was the only class I had on Tuesday afternoons was a problem.

I was working nights (from 6:00 p.m. to 12:30 a.m.), and after sleeping most of the day I hated having to go downtown for a 3 o'clock class and then rush back uptown to get to work on time. I was putting more value on my paycheck than my education. I used to say that if school would pay me I would go more often.

The biggest problem was that I didn't feel like I was experiencing college life. Baruch didn't have dormitories, a large campus, or the feel of college. Most of the people there, myself included, just went in, went to class and then went to work. But that wasn't what I wanted.

I wanted to live on a campus away from my usual environment. I wanted school to be my life for four years. I wanted to eat, sleep, and party in or around my campus. I wanted to feel connected to the other students. But most of the people who attend

CUNY schools are too busy trying to support themselves while educating themselves to have time to experience each other.

Since I wasn't getting what I wanted out of college, I quickly grew tired of working long and hard just to pay for books and that ridiculous tuition. To make a long story short, I ended up leaving school in the middle of my first semester, after only three months.

It wasn't until I left school that I realized why I failed at one of the most crucial challenges of my life. I think I set myself up to fail because I never dreamed of going to school in the city. I had always imagined myself on a college campus away from everyone and everything I had grown accustomed to during the last 19 years of my life. So when I had to attend a city school, failing was my way of rebelling.

I realize now that I am cut out for college—just not the college I ended up at.

I came to the conclusion that I wasn't ready for college, or maybe I was too lazy. After I left school, I continued working as a telephone interviewer with full-time hours. It wasn't a difficult job. All I had to do for eight hours a night was call people across the nation and type their answers to surveys into a computer. But I felt like my life was worthless.

When I was in school I felt a little productive, but now all I did was work all night and sleep all day. I felt like I was wasting my pitiful life away. My job wasn't even stable—there wasn't always a lot of work, so I couldn't rely on my checks being the same amount every payday.

I finally quit, thinking I could find a better job and start to make a decent living for myself until I was ready to go back to school. Truthfully, I didn't really want another job, but I did want money to buy the things I needed and to support my social life. The problem was that most jobs asked for both a college degree and a lot of skills. Even though I had some skills, I didn't have a college education. It's too bad I couldn't get paid for watching talk shows every morning.

Talk shows can fill up your day, but I was bored and sinking deeper into depression. After a month or two of unemployment, I told myself that there was no way for me to have the things I want in life without college.

I realize now that I am cut out for college—just not the college I ended up at. Right now, I'm trying to get into a SUNY school. That way I'll be able to live on campus the way I always imagined I would. Now that I've experienced first-hand what it's like to live in one place, work in another place, and go to school someplace else, I'm more convinced than ever that I need to eat, sleep, and breathe college in order to succeed.

Troy was 20 when he wrote this story. He went back to college and graduated from SUNY Purchase, then got a master's degree in education administration and became a high school principal.

Rudá Tillet

Take Our Advice: Managing Your Time

"I took a class with a woman who has three kids and works a full-time job, and she still goes to school. So I know if she can do that and get good grades, then I can certainly do it."

—*Pauline*, 21, *junior*

"I write everything in my planner. I can't function without one. I always transfer everything from the syllabus to my planner, otherwise I'll forget."

—*Janill*, 21, *senior*

"When I get home, I shower, eat, lie down and read. And in the morning I'll come to work a little early or stay a little later and read up."

—*Hector*, 22, *sophomore*

"In our dorm rooms, our closet doors are made out of mirrors, so I just wrote everything I had to do on the mirror with a dry-erase marker. It washes off. I see it every morning when I open my closet. It's a good system."

—*Tasha*, 20, *sophomore*

"At first I became so overwhelmed with my assignments that it began to wear me down. I've handled it by going to study hall and using my free time to study. Why fight with yourself when you could get the help that's right under your nose in the study hall, the tutoring center, or college library?"

—*Ashunte*, 20, *freshman*

"It's obvious who is and who is not studying. You'll realize that when you see your class shrinking, when you see the same people come in late to class or leave class early like they did in high school. Don't be one of them."

—*Pedro*, 21, *sophomore*

"I fixed my time management problem by using a planner where I arranged my appointments, my classes, and my free time. A friend also gave me a great piece of advice: do your college assignments during times of day when you feel energetic, and save e-mails, MySpace, and Facebook for right before you go to bed when you feel exhausted."

—*Teyu*, 18, *freshman*

Jessica Deng

Community College:
A Second Chance

By Jordan Temple

I used to think community colleges were just a fallback option if you completely bombed in high school. That's kind of what happened to me, actually. I attended four different high schools over four years, and I chose to clown around instead of doing my work. I was a know-it-all with false confidence. I felt that because of my strong grades in middle school and freshman year of high school, I was in the clear to meander through the halls instead of attending class.

I finally got my act together a year and a half ago at my fifth high school, a school that helps kids catch up on their credits and improve their grades. If it wasn't for that school, which pulled me in and helped me graduate, I'd probably be in a dead-end job right now instead of pursuing a career.

I knew that I wanted to go to college last year when I started getting my grades up. I felt better about myself and I had a good sense of what I should be doing—furthering my education. Over a year and a half, I worked to earn credits and improve my grades, and I finally graduated from high school.

When my guidance counselor suggested I look through the State University of New York handbook to see which two-year colleges I might like to attend, I felt regretful that I didn't have the grades to go to a four-year college.

I felt like I'd been given a clean slate. Now I could be an individual instead of keeping up my slacker image.

But I was glad I could attend college, period. I figured that if I worked hard and managed my money, I could transfer to a four-year college and leave with my BA, accumulating less debt than I would have if I'd gone to a four-year college the whole time. And as it turned out, community college has been a great start for me.

I was relieved when I found out that some community colleges had dorms, because I wanted to get out of the city, meet new people, and get the entire college experience. I wanted fresh air and a change of scenery, away from the distractions of city life and friends.

I eventually settled on Onondaga Community College in Syracuse, one of the largest community colleges in central New York. There are 9,000 day students and 500 students who live in dormitories. The college's website and virtual tour of the dorms blew me away, and so did the quality of the professors.

I met professors at an open house and that made it that much easier for me to choose Onondaga over the three other community colleges where I was accepted. I was interested in communications, and the teachers explained what courses would benefit me and what careers I could pursue (marketing, public relations,

English teacher, journalist, etc.) with the major. Plus, my credits would easily transfer to a four-year college after two years.

When I first got there last January, I was really shy and kept to myself. But I grew to like living in the dorms and meeting people. Students were nice. They held doors for each other from, like, 20 feet away and said hello.

I also liked the academic scene. I felt like I'd been given a clean slate. Now I could become more of an individual instead of keeping up my slacker image.

I took four classes my first semester: Interpersonal Communication, English, Oceanography, and College Learn Study, a class about college study habits. My professor for that class, Professor Prettyman, was stern but cool. He was a middle-aged African-American whose Afrocentricity rivaled my mother's.

He had posters of Malcolm X in his office and wore dashikis (traditional African clothes) to class. We spoke about my grades (and sometimes my effort in his class; he called on me all the time!), what classes I enjoyed, my major, issues in the black community, and my favorite sport, baseball. It was nice to have a professor I could talk to.

I found ways to have intercultural communication as well. I was interested in clubs that brought people together. At Onondaga, I found two that did just that. I joined the English-as-a-Second-Language mentoring program, where an American-born student is paired with an international student. They meet twice a week to share their cultures, opinions, and questions, and to talk about college life.

I was paired with Seung Young Kim, a student from Korea. We talked about the difference between North and South Korea, Korean celebrities, and America's favorite pastime (and mine): baseball. We became good friends and learned a lot from each other.

I also joined the JAAMA club, a club that promotes unity among African-Americans on campus and shares ideas about issues in the black community. In the fall, I'm going to run for student representative, which would mean I'd be responsible for getting money for the club at student government meetings and recruiting more people to join.

Most importantly, I figured out my study habits. I found that the library is where I am most focused, and I practically lived there my first semester. My plan is to get my grades up and then transfer to a four-year college. Many Onondaga students transfer to Syracuse University after two years, and I hope that I can do the same.

Even if I don't get into Syracuse, I want to attend a four-year college that has a good speech communications program, a marketing and business program, and a center for aspiring entrepreneurs. One day I'd like to become a baseball scout and, eventually, general manager of a baseball team. I also want to

If I worked hard and managed my money I could transfer, accumulating less debt than at a four-year college.

start a non-profit to fund low-income kids to go to baseball camp. I want to start an initiative to get more blacks back in baseball— in front offices, on major league teams, playing abroad, scouting and playing minor league ball. A background in business and marketing would help me with that.

But for now, my focus is school. This fall I hope to maintain a 3.3 GPA or higher. I also would like to be more outgoing and attend more school events, go to a party or two, and contribute to a poetry slam. I developed a passion for writing poems my first semester. I thought a lot at school, and I started wanting to write down my thoughts (in between essays and homework).

I'm glad I embraced the idea of community college even though I had my doubts about it at first. College has been a great experience so far. I feel a lot more at peace with myself now. I know who I am: a kid who loves to read and learn new things and is obsessed with baseball. I can see the purpose in everything that I do now, and how doing well in the present will help solidify my future. Community college hasn't been a disappointment, but a second chance.

Jordan was 20 when he wrote this story.

Take Our Advice: Making the Most of Academics

"As I began to read more in college, my vocabulary increased. Now I can comprehend what I'm reading better and I have a clearer idea of how to write. The more you read, the more you will understand words and how to put them together in the right form."

— *Pedro*, 21, *sophomore*

"Build a relationship with your teachers. If you're having trouble, go to them and say, 'OK, I know I'm failing and I know I have to pick up the slack. How can I do this?' Some teachers say if you fail you fail. But if you build up a relationship with them, there's more of a chance you can do it. If you don't make yourself known, they're not going to know you. I don't shut up in class now."

— *Hector*, 22, *sophomore*

"Lecture halls are huge, and sometimes you don't hear well in the back. I always try to stay right at the front so that I can hear the professor. Lecture can also be intimidating when you don't understand something. In my mind, it was like, 'I don't really want to ask something in front of 300 people when it might be an obvious thing.' But as semesters went along, I got better and better at it. I didn't really care. It's my grade; I ask whatever I want."

—Janill, 21, senior

"I advise forming study groups because learning as a group and asking questions is more effective than just reading the textbook over and over again. You're more likely to understand the concepts and less likely to fall asleep when you interact with others."

—Teyu, 18, freshman

"Going to a professor's office hours is the best way to get help. Not only will you get answers straight from the source, it tells your professor that you are taking the class seriously and you are doing your best."

—Te-Li, 20, junior

"If there are any doubts in your mind when you're trying to pick a major—and there will be lots of doubts as to what you want to do—talk to your academic adviser. That was really helpful to me."

—Desiree, 19, sophomore

Study Strategies

Keeping up with readings

When you're reading, don't just highlight! Instead:

1) Outline as you read. Begin by skimming through the reading to see what the major topics and sub-sections might be. Then read the material more slowly than usual and write your outline of the major points as you read along.

OR:

2) Break down the reading material into smaller, more digestible sections. After each small section, close the book and write down what the important points are (in your own words). Before going on to the next section, reread to check your facts and to be sure you didn't miss anything. This method allows you to read whole sections without having to stop to write your outline. Have a dictionary handy to look up the meaning and pronunciation of words you're unfamiliar with.

Prepping for exams

1) Organization: Make sure you are keeping up with the weekly readings. Organize your notes from class and from your readings. Don't rely on just one or the other; incorporate both.

2) Form study groups of three to four people. Take turns assuming the role of "teacher," explaining certain points to the others in the group.

3) Flash Cards: Write the word/concept/idea on one side of an index card and write the definition/explanation/

example on the other side. Then test yourself as you are waiting on line, on lunch breaks, on the bus, etc.

4) Studying: Do NOT cram the night before. Start studying as early as possible. Take advantage of professors' office hours if you have any questions, as there may not be time for review during class.

Eduardo Marquez

Minnesota Merengue

By Kizzy Charles-Guzman

When I announced last spring that I was going to attend Carleton College in Minnesota, a private school that's only about 10% black and Hispanic, my friends nearly passed out. I received all sorts of advice, warnings, and words of encouragement.

My favorite was: "Just keep in mind that you're going there to study, not necessarily to make friends. So if they don't want to befriend you because of your race, don't you mind them. Keep your nose in your books. Know what I'm sayin'?"

Even though I was sure Carleton wouldn't be that bad, and I'm used to interacting and relating to people of different races, I admit that I was nervous about attending a "white" college. My friends swore that I was doomed. But to my relief, going away to a mostly white college has been a very rewarding experience.

Yes, there are very few minorities in my school and I wish that the number of students of color who go away to white colleges would increase. I have always thought that more minorities should be empowered in America, especially through education.

Many people of color I know believe that minority students attending white colleges feel very uncomfortable, but white colleges will continue to be white colleges unless minority students start applying to and attending them. It will be a different experience, like realizing that there is a lot more beyond the cities where they've lived all their lives, but it doesn't have to be uncomfortable. I don't feel uncomfortable at all at Carleton, because people accepted me and made me feel like I belong.

This may be partly because I have not had the upbringing—or outlook on race—that the average American teenager has. I lived in Venezuela for 15 years before my family moved to New York. My mother is a light-skinned Venezuelan and my father is black, from Trinidad.

In Venezuela, most of my school friends were white. They were the children of Spanish and Portuguese immigrants and we all attended the same private Catholic school. Unlike my school, my neighborhood had all complexions: black, white and everything in between.

White colleges will continue to be white colleges unless minority students start applying and attending them.

Although we are all Hispanic in Venezuela, race is still an issue. Most people are dark-skinned, but in general the lighter you are, the better your position in society is. Over there, being light-skinned is considered a sign of prosperity because a lot of immigrants from Spain, Portugal and Italy came to Venezuela and eventually established businesses. In other words, the upper class in Venezuela is usually white.

So in Venezuela, I was aware of race, but since I never had any racist experiences it was not a big deal for me. That all changed when I moved to Brooklyn and I realized that, because of the great racial diversity, everything seemed to be turned into a race issue.

Most of my friends were either black or Hispanic, and they always wanted to show me how racist America was. They had been born in the U.S. and, having lived all their lives in poor neighborhoods in Brooklyn, they learned to be aware of the inequality of the races. To me, it seemed like they spent their lives looking for, and finding, signs of racism rather than uplifting one another and reaching out for a better life through education.

They were always reading into small things, like when we went out one day and got into an elevator where there was an elderly white lady. Everyone thought that she gave us "funny" looks and grabbed her purse, afraid of us because of our race. Quite honestly, I did not see her do such things, but hey, majority ruled. Maybe they were right. Maybe I was unaware of my surroundings.

When the college application process came around, I applied mostly to private schools because I needed a scholarship. (Many private schools offer scholarships for low-income and minority students because they want a more diverse student population.). I didn't pay attention to the schools' minority rates until after I applied. All I knew is that I wanted to go away.

But by the time I got on the plane to fly to Minnesota, I was convinced that I was going to hell. I had come to expect a bleak place where everyone would be mean to me because of my race.

During the first day of orientation, I walked into a room with about 200 students, almost all of them white. My first thought was, "Wow, I don't have blue eyes. What do I do now!?"

As the days went by, I noticed walking around campus how few minority students there really were. Blacks made up less than 7% of the students and Hispanics made up about 5% of them. In some classes I was one of two or three students of color.

I couldn't help but notice how "white" the school was, but everyone was so nice to me that I felt very comfortable within a few minutes. The other students would always smile and talk to me. Freshmen were always happy to talk about "how they ended up in Carleton," and invariably, we ended up knowing someone else's life story by the end of the night.

It helps that my roommate and I are also really close. My friends at home are surprised because my roommate is white and loves just about every sport, while I consider exercising a punishment. Still, we get along very well.

Not only were the people in the school nice, everyone in town was too good to be true. Strangers always smile at you and say hello when you pass them by in the streets. People are always willing to help you and give you information, and, get this, if you ask them for directions, they will often walk you to where you're going if it's nearby. In New York, all we get from people in the streets is attitude, rudeness, and catcalls.

When I arrived on campus I never thought about hanging out only with the other students of color, despite having been told that white people wouldn't really want to be my friends. I only thought of being myself, and if people liked me, they would accept me. I never felt that I had to reach out to white people or that I had to lay out my culture to them so that they would "learn" from me.

What I did notice was the attitude of the students of color. Most of them had grown up in large cities like Chicago and Los Angeles where the minority rates are much higher. Most of them had lived in segregated neighborhoods or attended segregated high schools. That made them feel a little out of place at Carleton.

For example, the students from L.A. were used to living in Hispanic neighborhoods and had only had black or Hispanic friends, so being around so many white people was foreign to them. As minorities, the students of color at Carleton feel that we need to stick together since there are so few of us.

They don't always say it's just because of race; one of my friends from L.A. says she spends so much more time with the other students from L.A. because they "have had the same experiences." She grew up in the same neighborhood as a couple of them and feels a strong connection to them.

She hangs out with me sometimes because I'm also Hispanic, but she thinks I can't even relate to her as well as her friends from L.A. You see, I don't have Mexican parents who moved to that particular neighborhood, so I don't really know "where she's coming from."

> *I do hang out with the students of color, but being around them is not all I want to do.*

Most of the minority students have views similar to my friend's. They don't want to learn from other people; they want to hold on to their own cultures. They want to join only culture-related clubs, leave the parties as soon as the DJ plays country or alternative music, and sit around complaining about the lack of minorities on campus.

I do not agree. Maybe because of my background, I see things differently. So I don't stick to one crowd at Carleton. I have a lot of friends of all races. I've joined clubs based on my interests, not on race. I'm even developing a taste for country music.

I don't want to take away from my college experience by being exclusive about the people I become friends with. Instead, I enjoy seeing how people can relate even when they come from different backgrounds. I like that I can see our cultures mixing in small ways, like when I came back from a meeting and there were about nine people hanging out in my room, listening to my salsa tapes, even though six of the people were white.

That night we just talked and joked around and all we listened to was Latin music and some reggae. I was intrigued that they had chosen my music, so I asked them why they were listening to salsa and they just said, "Because we like it." Later, I felt really stupid that I had asked.

I love Carleton. I'm glad that I get to experience life around both white people and students of color. I do hang out with the students of color, but being around them is not all I want to do.

This is America and whites are still the majority in this country. Chances are that my future bosses will be white, so why should I be scared of white people? I'm not denying that there is racism in the world. I just think that, especially when we go away to college, we should appreciate all cultures and make an effort to cross, not create, barriers.

Kizzy was 19 when she wrote this story.

Take Our Advice: Dealing with Distractions

"My extracurricular activities distract me. All the clubs seem so awesome. It's good to get involved in campus groups, but at the same time you really have to focus on your schoolwork."

—*Janill*, 21, *senior*

"Dorm life can be a distraction. There are always people around. At 3 a.m., you have a paper to write and everyone's just so interesting. My room was right outside the elevator so everyone came barging in all the time. It was really hard to get stuff done. I had to sneak away to the library."

—*Desiree*, 19, *sophomore*

"Parties! You get all these party invites and you're like, 'Yeah! I'm gonna go clubbing and I'm gonna write this paper tonight—of course I can do that!' You can't do that.

—Tasha, 20, sophomore

Females are much different in college than they were in high school. They know what they want to achieve in life. They don't focus on boys and MySpace, they don't have loud outbursts, and they have a greater vocabulary as well as vision for their lives. They motivate me, but it's distracting because I start focusing on them instead of class.

—Pedro, 21, sophomore

Teens:
How to Get More Out of This Book

Self-help: The teens who wrote the stories in this book did so because they hope that telling their stories will help readers who are facing similar challenges. They want you to know that you are not alone, and that taking specific steps can help you manage or overcome very difficult situations. They've done their best to be clear about the actions that worked for them so you can see if they'll work for you.

Writing: You can also use the book to improve your writing skills. Each teen in this book wrote 5-10 drafts of his or her story before it was published. If you read the stories closely you'll see that the teens work to include a beginning, a middle, and an end, and good scenes, description, dialogue, and anecdotes (little stories). To improve your writing, take a look at how these writers construct their stories. Try some of their techniques in your own writing.

Resources on the Web

We will occasionally post Think About It questions on our website, www.youthcomm.org, to accompany stories in this and other Youth Communication books. We try out the questions with teens and post the ones they like best. Many teens report that writing answers to those questions in a journal is very helpful.

How to Use This Book in Staff Training

Staff say that reading these stories gives them greater insight into what teens are thinking and feeling, and new strategies for working with them. You can help the staff you work with by using these stories as case studies.

Select one story to read in the group, and ask staff to identify and discuss the main issue facing the teen. There may be disagreement about this, based on the background and experience of staff. That is fine. One point of the exercise is that teens have complex lives and needs. Adults can probably be more effective if they don't focus too narrowly and can see several dimensions of their clients.

Ask staff: What issues or feelings does the story provoke in them? What kind of help do they think the teen wants? What interventions are likely to be most promising? Least effective? Why? How would you build trust with the teen writer? How have other adults failed the teen, and how might that affect his or her willingness to accept help? What other resources would be helpful to this teen, such as peer support, a mentor, counseling, family therapy, etc?

Resources on the Web

From time to time we will post Think About It questions on our website, www.youthcomm.org, to accompany stories in this and other Youth Communication books. We try out the questions with teens and post the ones that they find most effective. We'll also post lessons for some of the stories. Adults can use the questions and lessons in workshops.

Teachers and Staff:
How to Use This Book in Groups

When working with teens individually or in groups, you can use these stories to help young people face difficult issues in a way that feels safe to them. That's because talking about the issues in the stories usually feels safer to teens than talking about those same issues in their own lives. Addressing issues through the stories allows for some personal distance; they hit close to home, but not too close. Talking about them opens up a safe place for reflection. As teens gain confidence talking about the issues in the stories, they usually become more comfortable talking about those issues in their own lives.

Below are general questions to guide your discussion. In most cases you can read a story and conduct a discussion in one 45-minute session. Teens are usually happy to read the stories aloud, with each teen reading a paragraph or two. (Allow teens to pass if they don't want to read.) It takes 10-15 minutes to read a story straight through. However, it is often more effective to let workshop participants make comments and discuss the story as you go along. The workshop leader may even want to annotate her copy of the story beforehand with key questions.

If teens read the story ahead of time or silently, it's good to break the ice with a few questions that get everyone on the same page: Who is the main character? How old is she? What happened to her? How did she respond? Another good starting question is: "What stood out for you in the story?" Go around the room and let each person briefly mention one thing.

Then move on to open-ended questions, which encourage participants to think more deeply about what the writers were feeling, the choices they faced, and the actions they took. There are no right or wrong answers to the open-ended questions.

Open-ended questions encourage participants to think about how the themes, emotions, and choices in the stories relate to their own lives. Here are some examples of open-ended questions that we have found to be effective. You can use variations of these questions with almost any story in this book.

—What main problem or challenge did the writer face?

—What choices did the teen have in trying to deal with the problem?

—Which way of dealing with the problem was most effective for the teen? Why?

—What strengths, skills, or resources did the teen use to address the challenge?

—If you were in the writer's shoes, what would you have done?

—What could adults have done better to help this young person?

—What have you learned by reading this story that you didn't know before?

—What, if anything, will you do differently after reading this story?

—What surprised you in this story?

—Do you have a different view of this issue, or see a different way of dealing with it, after reading this story? Why or why not?

Credits

The stories in this book originally appeared in the following
Youth Communication publications:

"No More Hand Holding," by Edgar Lopez, *New Youth Connections*, September/October 2008; "The Army's Not For Me," by Roderick Scarlett, *New Youth Connections*, May/June 2001; "University of Kitchen?" by Orubba Almansouri, *New Youth Connections*, March 2009; "My Sister's Courage," by Wendy Kwan, *New Youth Connections*, May/June 1994; "From Failure to College," by Tanisia Morris, *New Youth Connections*, April 2006; "Beating the Odds," by Sayda Morales, *New Youth Connections*, September/October 2008; "My College Cloud," by Kenneth Douglas, *New Youth Connections*, January/February 2005; "So You Want to Go to College? Get Organized!" by Janill Briones, *New Youth Connections*, September/October 2006; "College Application Timeline," by Janill Briones, *New Youth Connections*, September/October 2005; "Bookin' It for the SAT," by Hattie Rice, *Represent*, May/June 2005; "How to Write a College Essay," by Esther Rajavelu, *New Youth Connections*, December 1995; "Choosing the Right College for You," by Anita Chikkatur, *New Youth Connections*, December 1995; "What to Ask When Choosing a College," by Latonya M. Pogue, *New Youth Connections*, December 1995; "I Want To Go To a Historically Black College," by Regina Haywood, *New Youth Connections*, December 2000; "Seeing for Myself," by Latonya M. Pogue, *New Youth Connections*, December 1995; "Are You Ready for Dorm Life?" by Magda Czubak, *New Youth Connections*, April 1995; "Getting Accepted is Only the Beginning," by Cassandra Lim, *New Youth Connections*, September/October 2008; "Financial Aid 101," *Represent*, May/June 2005; "There's Always a Choice," by Xavier Reyes, *Represent*, September/October 2008; "Take Charge of Your College Bills," by Marci Bayer, *New Youth Connections*, September/October 2008; "In My Own Hands," by Orlando Hawkins, NOT PUBLISHED (don't need to include?); "Freshman Year: A Fresh Start," by Ferentz Lafargue, *New Youth Connections*, April 1995; "My First Semester: Overworked, Underpaid, and Unprepared," by Troy Shawn Welcome, *New Youth Connections*, April 1995; "Community College: A Second Chance," by Jordan Temple, *New Youth Connections*, September/October 2008; "Minnesota Merengue," by Kizzy Charles-Guzman, *New Youth Connections*, January/February 1999.

About
Youth Communication

Youth Communication, founded in 1980, is a nonprofit youth development program located in New York City whose mission is to teach writing, journalism, and leadership skills. The teenagers we train become writers for our websites and books and for two print magazines: *New Youth Connections*, a general-interest youth magazine, and *Represent*, a magazine by and for young people in foster care.

Each year, up to 100 young people participate in Youth Communication's school-year and summer journalism workshops, where they work under the direction of full-time professional editors. Most are African-American, Latino, or Asian, and many are recent immigrants. The opportunity to reach their peers with accurate portrayals of their lives and important self-help information motivates the young writers to create powerful stories.

Our goal is to run a strong youth development program in which teens produce high quality stories that inform and inspire their peers. Doing so requires us to be sensitive to the complicated lives and emotions of the teen participants while also providing an intellectually rigorous experience. We achieve that goal in the writing/teaching/editing relationship, which is the core of our program.

Our teaching and editorial process begins with discussions

between adult editors and the teen staff. In those meetings, the teens and the editors work together to identify the most important issues in the teens' lives and to figure out how those issues can be turned into stories that will resonate with teen readers.

Once story topics are chosen, students begin the process of crafting their stories. For a personal story, that means revisiting events in one's past to understand their significance for the future. For a commentary, it means developing a logical and persuasive point of view. For a reported story, it means gathering information through research and interviews. Students look inward and outward as they try to make sense of their experiences and the world around them and find the points of intersection between personal and social concerns. That process can take a few weeks or a few months. Stories frequently go through 10 or more drafts as students work under the guidance of their editors, the way any professional writer does.

Many of the students who walk through our doors have uneven skills, as a result of poor education, living under extremely stressful conditions, or coming from homes where English is a second language. Yet, to complete their stories, students must successfully perform a wide range of activities, including writing and rewriting, reading, discussion, reflection, research, interviewing, and typing. They must work as members of a team and they must accept individual responsibility. They learn to provide constructive criticism, and to accept it. They engage in explorations of truthfulness, fairness, and accuracy. They meet deadlines. They must develop the audacity to believe that they have something important to say and the humility to recognize that saying it well is not a process of instant gratification. Rather, it usually requires a long, hard struggle through many discussions and much rewriting.

It would be impossible to teach these skills and dispositions as separate, disconnected topics, like grammar, ethics, or assertiveness. However, we find that students make rapid progress when they are learning skills in the context of an inquiry that is personally significant to them and that will benefit their peers.

When teens publish their stories—in *New Youth Connections* and *Represent*, on the Web, and in other publications—they reach tens of thousands of teen and adult readers. Teachers, counselors, social workers, and other adults circulate the stories to young people in their classes and out-of-school youth programs. Adults tell us that teens in their programs—including many who are ordinarily resistant to reading—clamor for the stories. Teen readers report that the stories give them information they can't get anywhere else, and inspire them to reflect on their lives and open lines of communication with adults.

Writers usually participate in our program for one semester, though some stay much longer. Years later, many of them report that working here was a turning point in their lives—that it helped them acquire the confidence and skills that they needed for success in college and careers. Scores of our graduates have overcome tremendous obstacles to become journalists, writers, and novelists. They include National Book Award finalist and MacArthur Fellowship winner Edwidge Danticat, novelist Ernesto Quiñonez, writer Veronica Chambers, and *New York Times* reporter Rachel Swarns. Hundreds more are working in law, business, and other careers. Many are teachers, principals, and youth workers, and several have started nonprofit youth programs themselves and work as mentors—helping another generation of young people develop their skills and find their voices.

Youth Communication is a nonprofit educational corporation. Contributions are gratefully accepted and are tax deductible to the fullest extent of the law.

To make a contribution, or for information about our publications and programs, including our catalog of over 100 books and curricula for hard-to-reach teens, see www.youthcomm.org.

About the Editors

Autumn Spanne is the editor of *Represent*, Youth Communication's national magazine by and for youth in foster care. Prior to working at Youth Communication, Autumn was a reporter for newspapers in Massachusetts and California and spent five years teaching English and journalism on the Navajo Nation. She has a BA in literature from the University of California, Santa Cruz, an MS in journalism from Columbia University, and an MA in education from Western New Mexico University.

Keith Hefner co-founded Youth Communication in 1980 and has directed it ever since. He is the recipient of the Luther P. Jackson Education Award from the New York Association of Black Journalists and a MacArthur Fellowship. He was also a Revson Fellow at Columbia University.

Laura Longhine is the editorial director at Youth Communication. She edited *Represent*, Youth Communication's magazine by and for youth in foster care, for three years, and has written for a variety of publications. She has a BA in English from Tufts University and an MS in Journalism from Columbia University.

More Helpful Books
From Youth Communication

The Struggle to Be Strong: True Stories by Teens About Overcoming Tough Times. Foreword by Veronica Chambers. Help young people identify and build on their own strengths with 30 personal stories about resiliency. (Free Spirit)

Starting With "I": Personal Stories by Teenagers. "Who am I and who do I want to become?" Thirty-five stories examine this question through the lens of race, ethnicity, gender, sexuality, family, and more. Increase this book's value with the free Teacher's Guide, available from youthcomm.org. (Youth Communication)

Real Stories, Real Teens. Inspire teens to read and recognize their strengths with this collection of 26 true stories by teens. The young writers describe how they overcame significant challenges and stayed true to themselves. Also includes the first chapters from three novels in the Bluford Series. (Youth Communication)

The Courage to Be Yourself: True Stories by Teens About Cliques, Conflicts, and Overcoming Peer Pressure. In 26 first-person stories, teens write about their lives with searing honesty. These stories will inspire young readers to reflect on their own lives, work through their problems, and help them discover who they really are. (Free Spirit)

Out With It: Gay and Straight Teens Write About Homosexuality. Break stereotypes and provide support with this unflinching look at gay life from a teen's perspective. With a focus on urban youth, this book also includes several heterosexual teens' transformative experiences with gay peers. (Youth Communication)

Things Get Hectic: Teens Write About the Violence That Surrounds Them. Violence is commonplace in many teens' lives, be it bullying, gangs, dating, or family relationships. Hear the experiences of victims, perpetrators, and witnesses through more than 50 real-world stories. (Youth Communication)

From Dropout to Achiever: Teens Write About School. Help teens overcome the challenges of graduating, which may involve overcoming family problems, bouncing back from a bad semester, or even dropping out for a time. These teens show how they achieve academic success. (Youth Communication)

My Secret Addiction: Teens Write About Cutting. These true accounts of cutting, or self-mutilation, offer a window into the personal and family situations that lead to this secret habit, and show how teens can get the help they need. (Youth Communication)

Sticks and Stones: Teens Write About Bullying. Shed light on bullying, as told from the perspectives of the bully, the victim, and the witness. These stories show why bullying occurs, the harm it causes, and how it might be prevented. (Youth Communication)

Boys to Men: Teens Write About Becoming a Man. The young men in this book write about confronting the challenges of growing up. Their honesty and courage make them role models for teens who are bombarded with contradictory messages about what it means to be a man. (Youth Communication)

Through Thick and Thin: Teens Write About Obesity, Eating Disorders, and Self Image. Help teens who struggle with obesity, eating disorders, and body image issues. These stories show the pressures teens face when they are confronted by unrealistic standards for physical appearance, and how emotions can affect the way we eat. (Youth Communication)

To order these and other books, go to:
www.youthcomm.org
or call 212-279-0708 x115

CPSIA information can be obtained at www.ICGtesting.com
Printed in the USA
BVOW04s0858201113

336749BV00008B/239/P